ADOBE® DIGITAL IMAGING
HOW-TOs

100 ESSENTIAL TECHNIQUES
FOR PHOTOSHOP CS5, LIGHTROOM 3,
AND CAMERA RAW 6

DAN MOUGHAMIAN

Adobe Digital Imaging How-Tos:
100 Essential Techniques for Photoshop CS5, Lightroom 3, and Camera Raw 6

Dan Moughamian

This Adobe Press book is published by Peachpit.

Peachpit
1249 Eighth Street
Berkeley, CA 94710
510/524-2178
510/524-2221 (fax)

For the latest on Adobe Press books, go to: www.adobepress.com
To report errors, please send a note to: errata@peachpit.com

Peachpit is a division of Pearson Education.

Editor: Rebecca Gulick
Production Editor: Hilal Sala
Project Editor: Robyn G. Thomas
Proofreader: Patricia Pane
Cover and Interior Designer: Mimi Heft
Indexer: Valerie Haynes Perry
Technical Reviewer: Shangara Singh
Compositor: codeMantra

ISBN-13: 978-0-321-71987-4
ISBN-10:   0-321-71987-5

9 8 7 6 5 4 3 2 1

Printed and bound in the United States of America

For my wife, Kathy. You are everything to me.

Acknowledgements

Many long hours have gone into this book. I'd like to sincerely thank the following editors for their many contributions, without which this work would not be possible: Rebecca Gulick, Patricia Pane, Hilal Sala, Shangara Singh, and Robyn Thomas. Regardless of the challenges that arose, be it figure formatting, technical considerations, or perfecting the copy, each brought expertise that was invaluable. It was a pleasure working with each of you.

To Victor Gavenda, thank you for the opportunity to be a part of this exciting series from Peachpit and Adobe Press. It's an honor to join this team of talented and dedicated authors!

Special Thanks

A big thank you to my family and close friends, who have continued to be supportive of my chosen career, and who always have good advice and many ideas for helping me to evolve as a professional. A special thank you to my parents for all they've done to help advance my career. Without each of you, I wouldn't be the man I am today.

Contents

Foreword

The year 2010 has been an exciting time for digital photographers and imaging professionals. The introduction of Photoshop CS5 and ACR 6, as well as Lightroom 3, brought many new capabilities and improvements. When I was offered the chance to put together 100 tips for these applications, I was excited. The trick, of course, is to narrow everything to just 100 tips when there are so many features and capabilities!

As I reflected on my own experiences (and those of other professionals in the Photoshop community), it seemed reasonable to break down the challenge by task. There are—essentially—four tasks that affect any digital photographer: getting pictures into the computer and organized; developing the raw data; perfecting files with Photoshop; and considering the output details. An author could focus all attention on any one of those tasks and easily create 50–100 tips.

I chose to focus most of the tips on developing raw files in Lightroom 3 (and by extension ACR), and on perfecting those files in different ways using Photoshop CS5. I hope that you will find the breakdown and relative "weighting" of the tips to be helpful, as you seek to get things done as efficiently and precisely as you can. As with most digital workflows, there are often several techniques for accomplishing any given task (such as color correction). Consider each of these tips, as well as those you may find elsewhere, to be your guideposts as you work with your images. There are few absolutes with digital imaging; it's all about finding the techniques that work best for your photography and your setup.

I hope that you get a lot of mileage from these tips and that the book can serve as a frequent reference in your work. Best of luck, and remember: There's a part of this amazing world out there waiting for you to discover and photograph, and it can't be done sitting in front of a computer. Like a camera or lens, software is just a tool for making the final product better. So get out there and go after it!

—Dan Moughamian

About the Author

Dan Moughamian has nearly 20 years of experience working with Adobe applications, including more than 16 years with Photoshop. He is a veteran of the Adobe alpha- and beta-testing programs, as well as an experienced photographer and professional instructor. Dan has authored a series of Adobe training tutorials, including *Image Retouching & Adjustment with Photoshop CS5 and Core Lightroom 3*. His articles have been featured in *photo technique* magazine, *Photoshop User Magazine*, and on Peachpit.com. You can follow Dan on Twitter @Colortrails.

CHAPTER ONE

Getting Organized with Lightroom 3

Organizing… the mere mention of it can send people running in the other direction. The word conjures images of day planners, curled-up post-it papers stuck to the base of your monitor, to-do lists etched onto a coffee shop napkin, even cleaning up the office! (No, that random pile of books and photo magazines with the lens set squarely atop does not constitute "organization," friend. An "advanced filing system" maybe, but not organization.)

As creative minds, keeping all of our media organized can be our biggest challenge. Put bluntly, organizing as a concept is rigid. It is—essentially—logical, repeatable structure. Unfortunately, as artists we don't think linearly, and we don't create linearly. Yet, "getting organized" often requires linear thinking. Proper categorizations, hierarchies, metadata, attributes: this is the stuff organization is made from. How else are we going to know what we're looking at eight months from now if we don't put those pictures in their place?

That's what this chapter is about: using the powerful and intuitive features in Lightroom 3 to organize all your images, so you can find and include them in your daily workflow more efficiently.

Why Lightroom?

I use Lightroom 3 to organize photos rather than Adobe Bridge, because it enables me to organize and then immediately begin editing my raw files in one elegant, unified interface. It is true that Adobe Bridge and Adobe Camera Raw (ACR) can—in combination—accomplish many of the same tasks as Lightroom, but in my opinion it requires more effort to set up the workspaces, manage the different modular windows, and edit my raw photos.

#1 The Lightroom User Interface

Lightroom 3 uses a simple, "digital darkroom" metaphor comprised of five application modules or modes: Library, Develop, Slideshow, Print, and Web. These modules are the real beauty of Lightroom, because the entire workflow fits neatly in one window. **Figure 1a** shows the access points for each of the five modules, near the top right part of the Lightroom window.

Figure 1a The Lightroom 3 user interface is divided into five primary modules or modes, seen at top right. They are Library, Develop, Slideshow, Print, and Web.

Library Module

The Library module is the primary focus for this chapter. The Library module in Lightroom 3 provides robust tools for importing photos; categorizing and applying attributes; comparing similar images in detail; and exporting files to new formats and workflows. The Library module is the photographer's best friend, making the linear process of organizing much easier.

The Library module uses four different view types: Grid view; Loupe view; Compare view; and Survey view.

Grid View

You can activate the Grid view by clicking the Grid icon, ▦ , or pressing the G key. This view presents all the photos in a selected folder as a series of thumbnails. You can resize each thumbnail, and each has a slide-like border that supplies additional information and controls for manipulating that file (**Figure 1b**). The Grid view is discussed in Tip #12.

Figure 1b The Grid view allows you to view all the photos in a folder as thumbnails.

Loupe View

If you need to view a large preview of your image in the Library module, use the Loupe view, by highlighting the image and pressing the E key (**Figure 1c**).

Figure 1c Select a thumbnail and press E to see a large preview of your photo.

Compare View

Compare view is designed to take two images that you select, magnify them, and place them side by side in the main preview area. To use this view, highlight your two chosen images and press the C key (**Figure 1d**). Compare view is discussed in Tip # 13.

Figure 1d Compare view allows you to make detailed comparisons of two similar images, side by side, in the main view area.

Survey View

Survey view works like the Compare view, except that you can place more than two images in the preview. It operates on principles similar to traditional lightboxes. To use this view, highlight the images and press the N key. (**Figure 1e**).

Figure 1e Survey view works like a small lightbox, allowing you to preview several images at the same time, at larger sizes than typical thumbnail settings.

Develop Module

The Develop module is where you control the exposure characteristics, contrast, color, and details of your photographs, as well as fix minor flaws caused by lens distortions.

Slideshow Module

Lightroom 3 provides options for creating slideshow presentations for clients and other interested parties, including robust formatting options.

Print Module

Lightroom 3 allows you to create customized photo packages (such as those used for school photos or athletic team photos) and contact sheets, again with robust formatting options.

Web Module

The Web module allows photographers to create web-friendly galleries of favorite photos, using simple templates and format options. You can find helpful tips for each of the Lightroom output modules—Slideshow, Print, and Web—in Chapter 3, "Lightroom 3 Output Hints."

#2 Maximizing Screen Space

Adobe has done well to fit all five workflow modules into a single, elegant user interface, but Lightroom can still use as much space as your screen will give it. To maximize your screen space, most of Lightroom's features and functions are divided into four panel groups within the main window. You can show or hide the left, bottom, right, and top portions of the interface independently.

For example, when you need to work in the Develop module for an extended period and won't be focusing on organizational tasks or other modules, you can collapse the panel groups you don't need to see. (**Figures 2a** and **2b**).

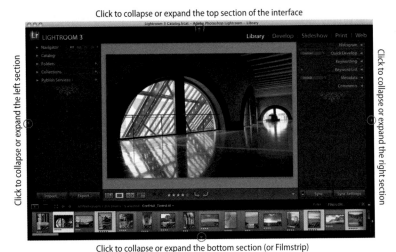

Click to collapse or expand the top section of the interface

Click to collapse or expand the left section

Click to collapse or expand the right section

Click to collapse or expand the bottom section (or Filmstrip)

Figure 2a Lightroom's various features and controls are divided among four sections (Top, Bottom, Left, and Right). Each can be collapsed individually by clicking the small triangles on the edges of the window.

This arrangement allows you to focus strictly on developing the exposure, contrast, color, and details in your image, without visual distractions. The same type of arrangement works well when organizing your photos or looking through files in the Library module.

Figure 2b After collapsing all sections except one and entering Full Screen mode, the Develop module is now completely focused on image-editing controls and a large preview.

Full Screen Mode

Lightroom also has a Full Screen mode that hides the operating system's window and menu bars, freeing up more space. You can cycle through the Lightroom screen modes by tapping the F key until you find one that suits your purposes.

Panel Quick-View

If you need to take a quick look at items in any of your four main panel groups, you can move the cursor over the edge of the panel, and it will be temporarily unhidden until you move the cursor away.

Lightroom Panels

Throughout this book and in other works you may see references to Lightroom *panels*. These refer to the individual groups of controls and features that reside within each section. For example, in the Develop module, the right side of the window houses panels like Tone Curve, HSL, and Details.

#3 IPTC Metadata Presets

Unless you're new to digital photography, you've probably heard about the importance of metadata. Metadata, put simply, allows you to "tag" image files with important information so that you can organize, find, and protect them more efficiently. However, entering IPTC (International Press Telecommunications Council) metadata (the type that includes information like captions, keywords, and copyright status) by typing in all the information, image by image, is a recipe for frustration (**Figure 3a**).

Metadata presets are a way to apply several pieces of IPTC information to many photographs at one time. For example, you may return from a shoot where you have several dozen "keeper shots" from the same location or point of interest. You can use a Metadata preset to simultaneously apply the same copyright, location, intellectual genre, keywords, and other values.

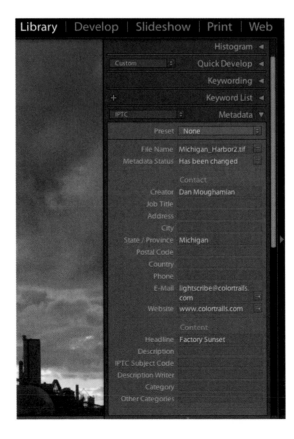

Figure 3a The IPTC metadata in Lightroom contains over 30 types of information that you can assign to any photo. Don't do it all by hand!

To create a new IPTC metadata preset for your workflow, try the following steps:

1. From the Library module, open the Metadata controls and choose IPTC from the Metadata pop-up menu (**Figure 3b**).

Figure 3b The Metadata panel offers access to several types of metadata.

2. From the Preset pop-up, choose Edit Presets (**Figure 3c**).

Figure 3c New metadata presets can be created from the Presets pop-up menu in the Metadata panel.

(continued on next page)

3. Scan the Edit Metadata Presets dialog box that appears, and fill in the values for the fields that will apply to all the images that will use the preset. As you enter the text for each item, the check box for that field will be selected automatically. If you are importing a large shoot, there may only be a half dozen or so values that will be identical among all the shots, but it's still worth setting up a preset (**Figure 3d**).

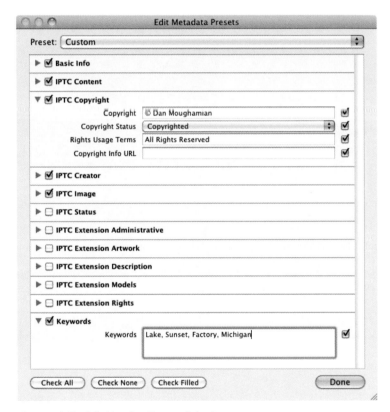

Figure 3d The Edit Metadata Presets dialog box.

4. When your criteria are filled out, click the Preset pop-up menu at the top of the Edit Metadata Presets dialog box, and choose Save Current Settings as New Preset. Give your preset a name in the New Preset dialog box and click Create (**Figure 3e**).

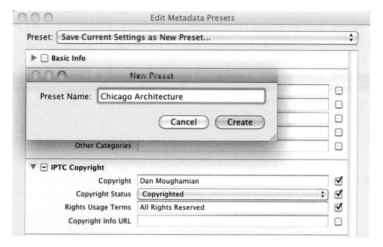

Figure 3e Give your preset a name that will make sense to you in the future.

Once you have created a preset, it will be available to use in the Photo Import dialog box, which is described next.

#4 Importing Photos with Metadata

Once you have created your metadata preset and you're ready to bring your latest shoot into Lightroom 3, head to the brand new Import window. You can access this window by clicking the Import button in the Library module (bottom of the left panel group), [Import...].

1. From the Source panel (left side of the Import window), choose the folder of images you wish to import by clicking it. This will show you thumbnail previews of all the images in the chosen folder (**Figure 4a**). By default, the check boxes for all the thumbnails will be selected.

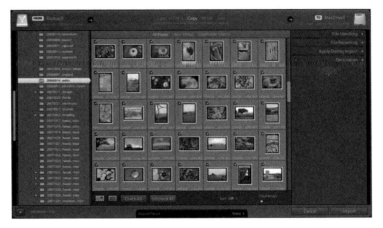

Figure 4a Lightroom 3's new Import window allows you to preview all the images in a folder or in a hierarchy of folders.

2. Deselect the thumbnail check boxes for any images you do not wish to import. This will dim the images unless you move the cursor over them, which will temporarily undim them (**Figure 4b**).

Figure 4b The new Import features make it easy to add only the images you need to your Lightroom catalog.

3. Choose the method of import (Copy as DNG, Copy, Move, Add) by clicking it (top center of the Import window). Once selected, a brief description of how it works will appear below the name of the method.

4. Set your File Handling options (top right), such as the Render Previews size and options to ignore suspected duplicates and make second copies (**Figure 4c**). To get the most accurate Render Previews while editing your files, choose Standard or 1:1.

Figure 4c Lightroom 3's Import File Handling options.

5. Open the Apply During Import panel, and using the Metadata pop-up menu, choose the preset you may have created. You can also apply Develop Settings and Keywords in this area, though I typically handle all raw edits later in the process (**Figure 4d**).

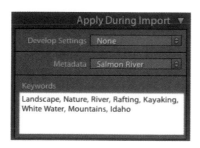

Figure 4d Lightroom 3's new Import features include the ability to apply Develop Settings, Metadata, and Keywords as files are being added to a catalog.

6. Click Import to add all the selected photos to your catalog. During import, Lightroom will display the thumbnails in the Library module and write all the metadata in your selected preset (and keywords) into your files.

#5 Renaming Folders

Managing Catalog Folders

If you're like me, after you spend a decent amount of time building up your new Lightroom 3 catalog, you'll need to periodically update the folders in Lightroom that you've created. Synchronization, hierarchy, and even renaming folders can play a role in staying organized. The trick is to know where to look. Intuitively, you might think the Folders pop-up or the Library menu are the places to look, but many of Lightroom's key organizational functions are tucked away in a convenient context menu.

To rename a folder in your Lightroom catalog, right-click the folder and choose Rename from the context menu (**Figure 5**). Note that changing the name of a folder in Lightroom will also change that folder's name at the system level.

Figure 5 To change a folder's name in Lightroom, you must right-click the folder and choose Rename from the context menu.

#6 Relinking a Moved Folder

Hard drives fill up; it's a fact of life for anyone who captures thousands of images or video clips. Another problem is that hard drive performance can taper off well before its capacity is reached. For these reasons, it can be a good idea to install another hard drive and move some of your projects and image folders to a new location.

However, if you move a folder that Lightroom has already imported as part of its Library, the application will not know where to find the folder contents and display a grayed-out icon with a question mark (**Figure 6a**). The same is true if you import photos from an external hard drive, which is later unplugged.

Figure 6a Lightroom won't update folders automatically that have been moved at the system level. Instead, it displays a question mark icon beside the folder.

Keep in mind that if you re-link Lightroom to a catalog folder located on an external hard drive, the link will remain active only as long as your Lightroom system is connected to that drive.

Fortunately, there is a simple remedy for this problem. Right-click the folder and choose Find Missing Folder (**Figure 6b**). This will open your system's file browser dialog box, so you can search for the folder's new location and select it to relink Lightroom and the folder contents.

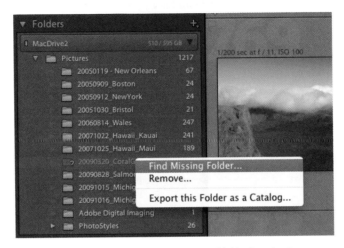

Figure 6b You can relink a catalog to a moved folder by using its context menu.

#7 Synchronizing Folders (New Images)

Another common occurrence for photographers is the need to add finished images or new originals to an existing folder in the Lightroom catalog. It's also common to remove images from an existing folder. To ensure the most up-to-date folder content is displayed, you need to synchronize Lightroom's "view" of the folder with what the system sees. To do this, right-click the folder that needs updating and choose Synchronize Folder from the context menu (**Figure 7a**).

Figure 7a Synchronizing catalog content starts by right-clicking the folder whose content has been changed since last using Lightroom.

This will open the Synchronize Folder dialog box (**Figure 7b**) that allows you to specify if you are scanning for new photos, removed photos, or metadata changes. Most often, I find it helpful to leave all three options selected, because it is easy to forget when I remove or add a single image to a folder or make edits to pictures in the folder, and then come back later to work in Lightroom.

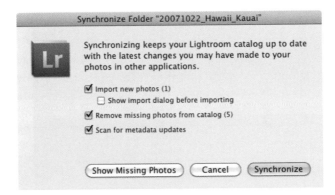

Figure 7b The Synchronize Folder dialog box allows you to choose which type of updates you'd like Lightroom to scan for when synchronizing.

Once you have synchronized the folder, the thumbnails in Lightroom's Library module will update, adding previews for any new files and removing previews of files no longer present (**Figure 7c**).

Figure 7c Once a folder is synchronized, Lightroom will update the Grid view, showing new thumbnails and removing those no longer present.

#8 Folder Import

Rather than manually synchronizing folder content that has been updated outside of Lightroom, sometimes it can be easier to import new images into an existing folder. To do this, right-click the folder you wish to add images into, and choose Import Into This Folder from the context menu (**Figure 8**). Once you do this, the Import window will appear, and you can choose your new images and import options as described in Tip #4.

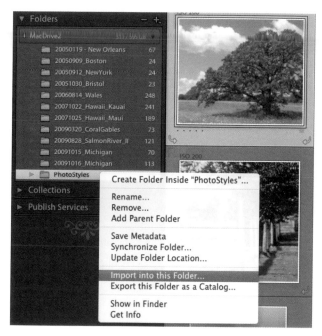

Figure 8 To Import additional files into an existing catalog folder, you can use the Import Into This Folder command from the context menu.

#9 Folder Export

For some situations (such as moving your Lightroom catalog to a new computer or sharing the catalog), it is necessary to export an entire folder and its contents (including subfolders) to a new location. To do this, you may first need to create a parent folder for all the folders in your hierarchy. This is typically the case if you store all your shoots in one master folder, but import them individually.

To create the parent folder, right-click any folder that is present in the top level of your master archive and choose Add Parent Folder from the context menu (**Figure 9a**). This will find the name of your master or parent folder automatically, and insert it at the top of your folder.

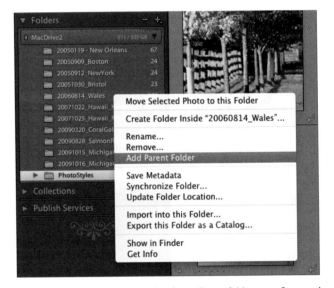

Figure 9a To create a new catalog from all your folders, you first need to create a parent folder (this is usually the master folder from which you import individual folders when creating your catalog initially).

Next, right-click the parent folder, and choose Export This Folder As A Catalog (**Figure 9b**). This will open the Export As Catalog dialog box, where you can choose to include or exclude the master negative files as well as the previews. From there you simply give the new catalog its name, choose a location, and save. Afterward, you can open Lightroom in your new environment and choose File > Open Catalog to locate your newly created catalog file and select it.

Figure 9b Export as Catalog allows you to choose options for your new catalog.

Excluding Negatives

Excluding negatives from a new catalog is typically done when you're trying to keep your catalog as compact as possible, so that you can quickly apply attributes or ratings. However, you will not be able to perform any edits or use other advanced features when reviewing your files from this type of catalog.

#10 Tethered Capture

Tethered Capture is new in Lightroom 3, addressing a long-standing request from photographers. This functionality allows you to connect a camera to the computer that is running Lightroom, view the basic exposure settings from within Lightroom, and activate the shutter release from Lightroom. Photos are then imported as they are taken. Anywhere your Lightroom laptop and camera can travel, you can capture images using the tether method. At the time of this writing, the cameras that support tethered shooting are:

Canon

- EOS 5D** and****
- EOS 5D Mark II
- EOS-1D Mark II* and**
- EOS-1Ds Mark II* and**
- EOS-1DS Mark III
- EOS-1D Mark III
- EOS-1D Mark IV
- EOS 7D
- EOS 450D (Digital Rebel XSi/ EOS Kiss X2)
- EOS 1000D (Digital Rebel XS/ EOS Kiss F)
- EOS 500D (Digital Rebel T1i/EOS Kiss X3 Digital)
- EOS 20D*** and****
- EOS 30D

- EOS 40D
- EOS 50D
- EOS 350D (Digital Rebel XT/EOS Kiss Digital N)****
- EOS 400D (Digital Rebel XTi/ EOS Kiss Digital X)

Nikon

- D3x
- D3s
- D3
- D700
- D300
- D300s
- D90
- D5000
- D200***

*These cameras only tether through a FireWire connection.

**Driver is not available for 64-bit Windows.

***These cameras are not supported on Windows.

****Camera needs to be set to PC connection mode to use the Tether feature.

For an up-to-date list of cameras supporting tethered shooting, check out http://kb2.adobe.com/cps/842/cpsid_84221.html.

To use Tethered Capture, use the following steps:

1. Choose File > Tethered Capture > Start Tethered Capture. This will open the Tethered Capture Settings dialog box (**Figure 10a**). Here, you can create a folder name for your captured shots by setting a Session Name, as well as set file Naming and Destination options, and Metadata Presets.

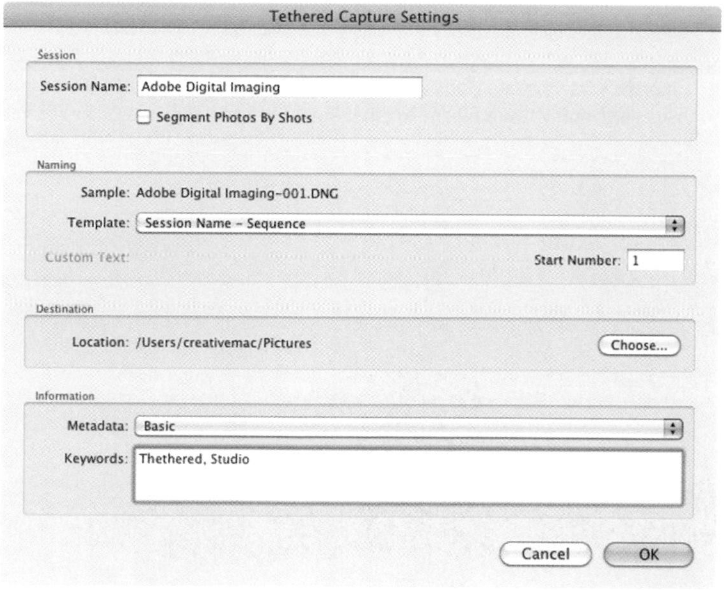

Figure 10a The Tethered Capture Settings dialog box allows you to set up your capture session.

Once you've created your settings and clicked OK in the Tethered Capture Settings dialog box, Lightroom will create a new empty folder in your catalog and display the Tether controller, which displays your camera model, shutter speed, aperture, ISO, white balance, and the option to apply a Develop preset to the images as you capture them.

2. Connect your camera and wait for Lightroom to recognize the connection.

(continued on next page)

3. All you need to do is click the Capture button in Lightroom or the shutter release button on your camera to take the picture (**Figure 10b**); the image will appear in your folder shortly thereafter with any metadata, keywords, and develop settings already applied. If you wish to change one of these settings, click the small cog icon at the bottom right of the Tether console.

Figure 10b Taking pictures with Tethered Capture just requires a click of the Capture button to activate your camera shutter and bring the image directly into your catalog.

#11 Increasing Speed: Catalog Optimization

For many photographers, it doesn't take long to fill up a catalog with thousands of images, many or all of which have metadata, keywords, attributes, develop settings, and other changes applied. After a time, this can slow Lightroom's performance, especially as you add and remove groups of new files.

To make sure Lightroom is running at its best, you can "rebuild" the Lightroom catalog files, ensuring all references and hard drive space are used as efficiently as possible, thus speeding up Lightroom. To do this, choose File > Optimize Catalog, and you will be greeted with a simple dialog box, asking you to confirm optimizing your catalog. Click OK and have your favorite online newspaper and beverage ready; it may take awhile (**Figure 11**).

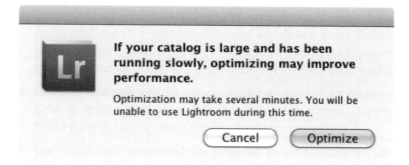

Figure 11 Optimizing your catalog (especially larger catalogs that have had many files modified, added, and removed) can improve Lightroom performance.

#12 Customizing the Grid View

The heart and soul of the Grid view are the photo thumbnails that act as a mini lightbox, showing you all the great shots and not-so-great shots in your active folder. However, Lightroom provides many options for customizing your thumbnails, allowing you to visually scan your images in more effective ways. To access these options, make sure you have the Grid view active and then click Command-J (Mac OS) or Control-J (Windows) to open the Library View Options dialog box (**Figure 12**).

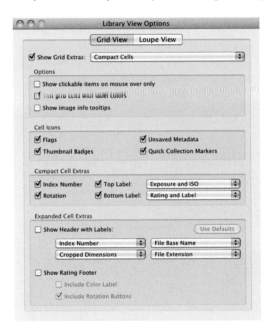

Figure 12 Using the Grid View Options wisely can ensure you maximize your screen space while having all the relevant information available to evaluate your photos.

Compact Cells

I'm a strong believer that for most Lightroom workflows, compact cells provide the best of both worlds. They allow you to see important attributes as well as key exposure data, while saving significant screen space.

Make sure the Show Grid Extras check box is selected (top left) so you can choose from among the different options available. Personally, I have a few favorites, and they revolve around using *compact (thumbnail) cells*. Cells are the slide-like borders that surround the thumbnail preview. The options I typically use are shown in Figure 12, with the results in the background. They include:

Options—Under the Options section, I choose to "Tint Grid Cells With Label Colors." This makes it easy to visually sort (and thus group) images by their label color.

Ratings and Labels—Under the Compact Cell Extras section, I use the Bottom Label pop-up menu to display the Rating and Label option for each cell. This not only allows me to see the Rating and Label of each shot, but also to set their values directly from the cell.

Exposure and ISO—Under the Compact Cell Extras section, I use the Top Label pop-up menu to display Exposure and ISO data for the cells. High ISO images require more detail work, which is covered in Tip #s 32 and 33.

Cell Icons—I use all these options to help me flag special shots, save changed metadata, and add other common tasks.

#13 Comparing Similar Photos

A critical task for any serious photographer is comparing photos with similar composition and exposure values, side by side, in order to determine which shot has the best detail and color. Lightroom excels at this task, and it's arguably the most important part of working in the Library module. After all, if you don't start with your best shots before moving to the Develop module, you may have already lost the battle. The first step is to select two similar images (**Figure 13a**).

Figure 13a Using the Grid view, select two image cells to begin your comparison.

Next, you need to jump into the Compare view by pressing the C key, or by clicking the button near the bottom of the Lightroom window, with the icon marked X|Y, ▦ ▭ X|Y ▦ . Once clicked, you will see your chosen images side by side in the main viewer (**Figure 13b**).

Figure 13b The Compare view makes it easy to pick the best image from a series of similar shots by zooming in to check their color, detail, and focus.

From this point, you have several options for controlling magnification, which images occupy which side of the preview, and the ability to apply attributes that identify which shots have been picked, flagged, or rejected. Take a look at some of the options that follow.

Magnification Options

Once you have two images side by side, zoom in and examine the details. The first order of business is comparing focus. If you have two shots that were taken at identical or nearly identical focal lengths and from the same vantage point, it's easiest to compare them using the same magnification. Lightroom sets this up by default by locking or *linking* the zoom for both images, Compare: 🔒 Zoom 1:1 .

Hidden Filmstrip

Remember that if you have the Filmstrip hidden and you need to access it while using the Compare view, just roll your cursor over the bottom edge of the window to temporarily activate it so that you can scroll through the thumbnails or select new shots.

30

Temporary Synching

If you would like to temporarily synchronize the magnification of two images without locking or linking their Zoom levels, right-click one of the images and choose Sync Focus in the context menu, or just click the Sync button, next to the Zoom slider, Sync .

You can use standard keyboard Adobe shortcuts to zoom into or out from the photos; or you can use the Zoom slider, and drag on either image to pan (or slide) them both in unison, to identify areas of differing focus, color, or detail. Some situations may require that you unlink the zoom magnification ratio for the two images. For example, this might be the case if you've photographed the same subject, from the same vantage point but with different focal lengths, or from a different distance but with the same focal length.

The end result is that in order to view the subject in both images that you are comparing at a similar level of magnification, you'll have to use different zooms. To do this, click the Zoom lock to unlock it, click on each preview, and zoom in or out independently (**Figure 13c**)

Figure 13c Zooming into each image independently helps when evaluating similar shots, where focal length or distance to subject vary. The image at left shows a 1:3 zoom ratio while the image at right shows a 1:2 ratio.

Swapping Photos

There are several ways of swapping out the images you are currently looking at with new shots, but the method I find most intuitive is what I call the "click and click" method (not the catchiest name ever, but it will do). Rather than use the automated switching controls, , and trying to figure out "who's on first," I use the following process with Grid view as my starting point:

1. Making sure no other cells are selected, choose two images and press the C key.

2. After you have made the comparisons, and you are ready to compare two new images, make sure the left side of the Compare view (called the *select* shot) is active by clicking it (look for the white highlight around the edge). (The image on the right side of the Compare view is called the *candidate*.)

3. Click a new image in the Filmstrip. This becomes the new select shot and the Filmstrip cell for this shot displays a small white diamond (upper-right corner).

4. Click the candidate photo on the right side of the Compare view (look again for the white highlight), then go to the Filmstrip and click a new image to replace it. Repeat this process as needed, selecting either the candidate or select shot, then using the Filmstrip to replace each.

Calling the Shots

The final step is to mark up "the winning photos" with attributes, so that if you have to walk away from Lightroom for a while and come back, you can pick up where you left off. There are two easy ways to mark your images with flags, labels, and ratings attributes.

- Right-click either photo, and choose Set Flag, and/or Set Rating, and/or Set Color Label, from the context menu to apply your settings (**Figure 13d**).

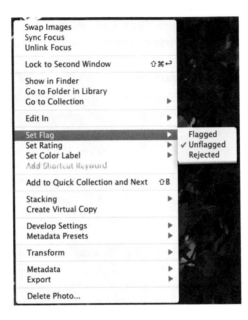

Figure 13d Right-clicking the select or candidate images in Compare view opens a context menu that makes it easy to flag, rate, or label the picture.

- At the bottom of both the select and candidate previews, are controls to set flags, ratings, and labels directly, by clicking the relevant settings for those options (**Figure 13e**).

Figure 13e You can also flag, rate, or label the select or candidate shots by clicking the built-in attribute controls, found directly under each image preview. From left to right: Flag status (white means flagged); Rating (3 stars); and (color) Label (yellow). Clicking the **X** will remove the image from the Compare view.

#14 One Attribute, Many Shots

Some situations dictate that you apply the same Color Label, Rating, or Flag attribute to a larger series of shots at the same time. The Grid view makes this a snap. For a contiguous series (or neighboring cells), click the first cell and then Shift-click the last cell to select all cells. (To select a noncontiguous range of cells, you can use Command-click on Mac OS or Control-click on Windows.) Next, right-click and choose Set Flag, and/or Set Rating, and/or Set Color Label from the context menu to apply your settings to all the selected images (**Figure 14**).

Figure 14 Apply attributes to many images at once by selecting multiple cells and right-clicking to access the context menu options.

Tip
You can also apply attributes to all the selected Grid view cells by clicking any one of the individual cell controls for Flags, Label Color, or Ratings. You can rotate multiple images in the same way, by using individual Rotate controls from an individual cell. You can also rotate images using keyboard shortcuts: Command–[rotates images counterclockwise, Command–] rotates images clockwise (Mac OS), while Control–[and Control–] perform the same functions on Windows.

#15 Using Keyword Sets

Suffice it to say entire books have been written on the subjects of keywords, metadata, and image management, so any attempt made here to compress it into a few simple tips would be folly. However, I have found that Lightroom has one tool in particular that makes it easy to work with keywords. Keyword sets reside in the Keywording section of Lightroom's Library module.

The principle behind them is that you create high-level categories of keywords, each of which contains nine specific topics relating to your custom category. You can create a new category by clicking the Keyword Set pop-up menu and choosing the Edit Set command (**Figure 15a**). Then set the nine keywords listed in the Edit Keyword Set dialog box (**Figure 15b**), and save them by choosing Save Current Settings as New Preset from the Preset pop-up menu.

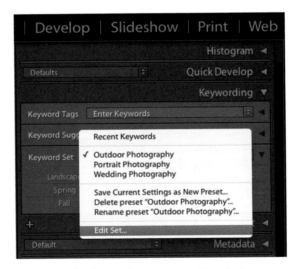

Figure 15a New keyword sets are created by selecting a default set and choosing Edit Set.

Figure 15b In the Edit Keyword Set dialog box, you can modify the nine keyword values, and then save them under a new name using the Preset pop-up menu at the top of the dialog box.

Using the keywords is a simple matter of choosing a keyword set from the pop-up menu, highlighting the photos you wish to apply keywords to, and clicking any keywords that apply from the list (**Figure 15c**). As you do so, the keywords are added to the image metadata.

Figure 15c Click a keyword from the Keyword Set list to apply it to your selected photo(s).

#16 Using the Library Filter

Once you have applied attributes, metadata, keywords, and other important information to the shots in your catalog, you may need to look across one or all of the folders in your catalog to find shots that have specific characteristics. The Library Filter (also called the Library Filter Bar) is a fantastic way to accomplish this task.

To activate the Library Filter Bar, look just above the top row of cells or thumbnails in the Grid view and choose a filter category (Text, Attribute, or Metadata), based on the search type you need to use. You can also press the Backslash key (\) or choose View > Show Filter Bar.

Text Filtering (Keyword Search)

For keyword searches, the Text filter works very well. Select the folder you wish to search, click the Text button, set the search category pop-up menu to Keywords and the secondary category to Contains, and type the keyword. The results automatically show up in the Grid view (**Figure 16a**).

Figure 16a Finding photos by keyword is simple using the Library Filter.

You can also search for IPTC metadata in your files using the same technique; just change the search category to Searchable IPTC from the pop-up menu.

Attribute Filtering

Want to pull together all images with a certain combination of Rating, Color Label, and Flag status? That's even simpler. Start with your search folder selected, click the Attribute button in the Library Filter Bar, and click the criteria icons you want to include. For example, you might want to show all images flagged as 4 stars or higher and labeled with blue or green (**Figure 16b**).

Figure 16b Use multiple attribute criteria to filter your photos by Flag status, Rating, and Color Label.

Filter Stacking

You can show all three filtering categories by clicking each category button in sequence, thereby "stacking" them into the Library Filter Bar. You can use combinations of Text, Attribute, and Metadata criteria for a single search! It is worth noting, however, that Keywords and Labels (for example) also fall under searchable metadata. Many combinations are possible.

Metadata Filtering

Metadata filtering allows you to use over a dozen file characteristics as search criteria, including:

- Aperture
- Camera model
- Focal length

- ISO
- Job
- Keyword

- Lens type
- Location
- Shutter speed

You can use as few as one and as many as eight metadata categories in your search. By default, Lightroom uses four. To open Metadata filtering and modify its categories, click the Metadata button, and then click and hold any column name to invoke a pop-up menu containing all the categories (**Figure 16c**).

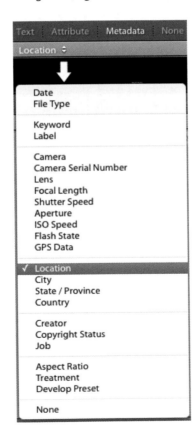

Figure 16c Each Metadata column can be assigned a specific category.

To add or remove a column from the list, mouse over the top-right corner of any column, click the icon that appears, and choose Add Column or Remove Column, ![menu].

Finally, you can click one metadata value in one or more columns (or Command-click on Mac OS or Control-click on Windows to select more than one value per column) to begin filtering your images by those criteria (**Figure 16d**).

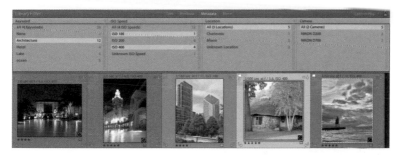

Figure 16d The Metadata Filter allows you to search using multiple criteria, including keywords and some attributes.

View Any Folder with One Filter

If needed, you can lock any custom Library Filter search that you create by clicking the new Lock button at the right edge of the Library Filter Bar, Custom Filter. This will ensure that regardless of which folder you click, the filtered view of its content will remain until you unlock the filter.

#17 Using Smart Collections

Many applications and operating systems use a *smart folder* concept today, Lightroom is no exception. The premise is that the contents of the folder are not based on the physical location of the files, but rather on the characteristics of the files. For this reason, *smart collections*—Lightroom's version of smart folders—are dynamic; their content changes as the images in your catalog change. This is similar to the filtering concepts we just mentioned, except that the filtering mechanism is the folder itself.

To access a collection in Lightroom, you'll need to open the Collections widget, located just below the Folders panel on the left side of the Library module (**Figure 17a**).

Figure 17a Smart Collections are a powerful and intuitive way to keep groups of your images organized based on different criteria.

When you click a smart collection, it acts as a filter and shows only the photos in your selected folder that meet the collection's criteria. You can start the process by clicking the Plus icon (+) and choosing Create Smart Collection from the pop-up menu (**Figure 17b**). This will open the Edit Smart Collection Dialog.

Figure 17b To create a Smart Collection, click the Plus (+) button and choose Create Smart Collection.

You can edit smart collection criteria by right-clicking the collection and choosing Edit Smart Collection from the context menu.

42

Once in the Edit Smart Collections dialog box (**Figure 17c**), you can set up your criteria by choosing a category and deciding whether or not to include certain values related to that category. You can create new categories and "stack them" (or remove a category) by clicking the Plus (+) or Minus (-) icons, respectively.

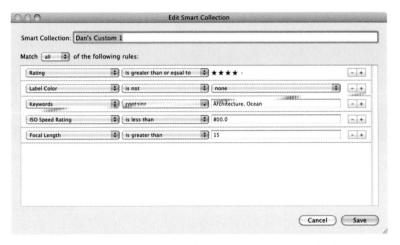

Figure 17c The Edit Smart Collections dialog box allows you to set multiple criteria for including and excluding photos from the collection. Lightroom evaluates these criteria in the background, as you work, adding or removing files as you change their characteristics.

To activate a smart collection, click its name in the Collections panel and all the images in your catalog that meet the criteria you selected in the collection will appear in Grid view.

CHAPTER TWO

Developing Raw Photos

Once your files are sufficiently organized, the next step in most workflows is to "develop" the raw files or digital negatives before moving them into Photoshop CS5 for detailed retouching, image adjustments, or other tasks. Adobe Camera Raw (ACR) and Photoshop Lightroom provide a nearly identical set of tools for developing and maximizing the image data captured by your camera.

The descriptions and screen shots in this chapter focus on Lightroom 3 and its Develop module. Although it is true that the combination of Adobe Bridge and ACR can accomplish most of the same organizational and raw editing tasks as Lightroom, the unified interface and extra refinement of the Lightroom 3 process have won me over. Whichever solution you choose, you should feel confident knowing that you have a very powerful set of tools at your disposal.

The important thing to remember as you read this chapter is that Lightroom 3 and ACR 6 (the latest version available at the time of this writing is version 6.1) accomplish every editing technique shown in the same way, using controls of the same type and name, unless otherwise noted. The only significant difference in most cases is the look of the user interfaces and the location of a few buttons and functions, such as previewing and output settings. Where there are substantial differences, you'll find ACR sidebars, plus a few ACR-specific tips at the end of the chapter.

#18 Understanding Process Versions

Lightroom 3 and ACR 6 offer several new features, but perhaps the most impressive are the improvements to capture sharpening and noise reduction. These processes are quite important to the raw editing process and are covered in Tip #32 and Tip #33, respectively, but the bottom line is you now can produce cleaner, sharper-looking images. However, because Lightroom and ACR handle image details in a new way, Adobe provides two paths for photographers who have used prior versions of these applications.

The first path provides continuity for those who need Lightroom 3 to handle their previously edited files in exactly the same way prior versions did; this is known as *Process 2003*. The applications also provide a path to upgrade previously edited files to the new standard; this is known as *Process 2010*. Here are some key points:

- Any file that is opened for the first time in Lightroom 3 will default to the new standard, known as *Process 2010*, giving you access to the new Noise Reduction controls and improved capture-sharpening algorithms.

- Any file edited with an earlier version of Lightroom that is subsequently opened in Lightroom 3 will display a warning icon, ⚡, alerting you to the difference in process version. Clicking this icon will reveal the Update Process Version dialog box (**Figure 18a**) that allows you to update a single photo to the new process version, preview the changes, and update the entire Filmstrip.

Figure 18a Lightroom 3 provides a dialog box allowing you to update the process version of your file (or files) with a few simple clicks.

- Any file edited in an earlier version of Lightroom or ACR that is opened in Lightroom 3, but not converted to Process 2010, will maintain its appearance and will subsequently use Process 2003. This in turn limits the number and type of controls that can be accessed for Noise Reduction and Sharpening edits (**Figure 18b**).

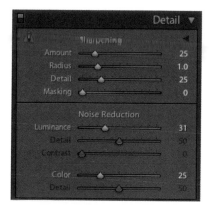

Figure 18b If you choose not to update the process version for files edited in older versions of Lightroom or ACR, the *new* Detail and Contrast controls for Noise Reduction will be inactive. Lightroom 3 will also use legacy sharpening processes in this case, although the same sharpening controls are available.

#19 Using Clipping Previews

One of my favorite features in Lightroom can be easy to overlook—namely, the ability to use the Histogram to show clipped shadow and highlight details in a photograph. To enable shadow and highlight clipping indicators, click the two small triangles at the top-left portion and top-right portion of the Histogram or press the J key. To disable them, click the triangles or press the J key a second time.

From this point, if you move any controls found in the Basic, Tone Curve, or HSL panels too far in one direction (either individually or in combination), areas of the image preview turn pure red if you've clipped the highlight details, or pure blue if you've clipped the shadow details (**Figure 19**).

Never Heard of Clipping?

Clipping occurs when the edits you're making to your raw file or DNG cause the darkest or lightest details in the image (or both) to shift to pure black or pure white, respectively. In effect, you lose all the detail in the darkest and/or lightest areas in your photo.

Figure 19 Clipping Previews can help to avoid overcorrection of the lightest and darkest details in your photos.

#20 Making Histogram Edits

Lightroom also allows you to use its Histogram to quickly modify the four primary tonal ranges that it depicts. From left to right, you can control Blacks, Fill Light, Exposure, and Recovery values. These values (and how they affect image quality) are covered in more detail in Tip #25. The Histogram in this example shows the Exposure region of the Histogram being highlighted (**Figure 20**).

To make Histogram edits, move the cursor over the tonal region you want to brighten or darken (this will cause it to "light up" slightly) then drag. Dragging to the left will darken the tones represented by that region of the Histogram; dragging to the right will brighten them. This method is visually intuitive and can help you to create a quick "first pass" on improving the overall exposure and contrast of your photo.

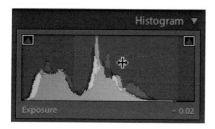

Figure 20 Adjust the distribution of tones in your image directly by dragging on the Histogram preview.

#21 Cropping and Straightening

The tools available in Lightroom provide intuitive and flexible controls for quickly improving photographic composition. Press the R key to display the Crop & Straighten controls (**Figure 21a**).

Straighten Tool

Lock Aspect Ratio

Figure 21a Lightroom 3's Crop & Straighten controls make it easy to tighten up your photos' compositions, so you don't have to add that step later in the editing process.

When it's necessary to ensure the final crop fits into a popular frame size or aspect ratio, I use the following steps:

1. Click the Aspect pop-up menu to assign the aspect ratio that best suits your photograph. Then click the Lock icon so that the ratio won't change as you manipulate the crop marquee.

2. If there is an obvious slant to the image, click the Straighten tool icon. This tool is located to the left of the Angle slider and looks like a golden level when you place the cursor over it.

3. Click and hold a point on the horizon (or on another object that you know to be horizontally level in the scene). Then move the cursor to a point on the opposite side of the horizon or object and release (**Figure 21b**).

Figure 21b The Straighten tool can remove unwanted camera rotation effects by dragging a line across the horizon or other level objects in the scene.

ACR Crop and Straighten

If you're using ACR, the Crop and Straighten functions are two separate tools on the ACR toolbar, ⬚⬚. However, clicking and holding the Crop tool will provide similar aspect ratio and constraint options (like Lightroom).

Lightroom will automatically rotate your image to straighten the shot (**Figure 21c**). This method often produces a good result more quickly than making a manual correction, which is done by dragging the Angle slider.

4. Once you finish straightening the image and you have applied the crop you want, pressing Enter or Return will accept the changes. But because it's a raw workflow, you can go back into Lightroom later, change the crop, and re-export your shot without altering the original pixels.

(continued on next page)

Figure 21c Lightroom automatically rotates the image to straighten it, once you have applied the Straighten tool.

#22 Removing Spots and Other Distractions

Dust spots, water spots, and small objects that detract from a picture are common occurrences in photography. The problem is not that the spots or distracting objects can't be removed in Photoshop CS5 (they can), but it's useful to show clients the shot previews as quickly as possible. To quickly identify unwanted spots, specks, hairline defects, or other unwanted small objects, use the following steps:

1. Zoom in between 50% and 100%. It should be easy to identify dust or water spots in areas of very consistent color or texture, like a blue sky, a portrait backdrop, or even on the side of a building or vehicle.

2. To remove small defects like these, press the Q key to display the Spot Removal controls and cursor (**Figure 22a**).

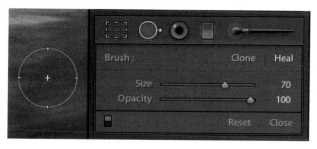

Figure 22a The Lightroom 3 Spot Removal Brush operates in two modes (Clone or Heal) and is designed to handle dust and water spots or other minor distractions in the scene.

You can choose to remove the spots in Clone or Heal mode, and choose the opacity value of the correction. Clone works much like the Clone Stamp tool in Photoshop. It will take one texture and replace it with another, while Heal will create a "hybrid texture" using the visual characteristics of both source and target area. Typically, I choose the Heal mode because it often provides a more natural-looking result.

3. To make a correction, set the size of the Spot Removal Brush cursor so that it is large enough to cover the entire defect.

(continued on next page)

Spot Removal Brush Shortcuts

Just as in Photoshop and ACR, you can optionally use the left and right square bracket keys to decrease or increase the size of your Brush cursor (that is, to define the diameter of the spot you're repairing). You can also press and hold the Command key (Mac OS) or Control key (Windows) and drag the Brush cursor out to its desired size.

ACR Spot Removal

The Spot Removal tool and settings in ACR work in a similar fashion to the Lightroom version, with a couple of differences. Instead of pressing the Q key to access the tools in ACR you click the B key or click the toolbar icon, 🖉 . Instead of changing settings between spot corrections, it's best to place the cursor over the defect first, then change the Brush size (which you can do easily by dragging the cursor) and the other options.

4. Place the Brush cursor over the defect, ensuring it doesn't overlap other areas that are important to the shot.

5. Click once and a second cursor appears that defines the source area with an arrow pointing toward the area being targeted (**Figure 22b**).

Figure 22b The Spot Removal tool provides two circular guides or cursors—one that covers the defect in the image, and one that defines the source area for repairing the defect.

6. Click inside the source cursor and drag, watching the preview of the defect area change as you move around the image. When you find a location that provides seamless-looking results, release the mouse button and the final result appears a second or two later. You can change Brush settings and follow the same process to clone over or heal other defects or distractions (**Figure 22c**).

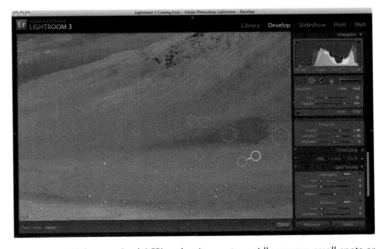

Figure 22c Lightroom (and ACR) makes it easy to rapidly remove small spots or distracting elements. Each circle here represents a spot-removal edit, in this case to remove small rocks and bright spots in the background.

#23 Synchronizing Spot Removals

Another common scenario photographers face is that they will find a series of photos that have the same spots, on the same locations. This most often is a result of water or dust spots on a particular lens. Rather than correct each shot manually, Lightroom makes it possible to synchronize spot removals.

To synchronize spot removals, follow these steps:

1. Find the first image where the spots occur and remove them as described earlier in Tip #22.

2. Press Command-C (Mac OS) or Control-C (Windows), or click the Copy button in the Develop module and make sure Spot Removal is selected (**Figure 23)** as well as any additional settings you want copied to other shots. (Steps for synchronizing edits in ACR are covered in Tip #38.)

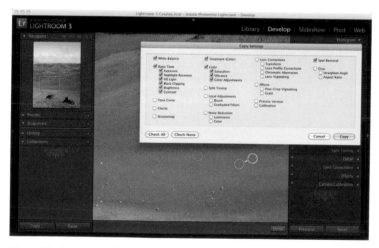

Figure 23 Spot removal corrections can by synchronized in Lightroom using the Copy (and Paste) functions.

3. Select the next shot (or shots) in the series from the Filmstrip, then press Command-V (Mac OS) or Control-V (Windows), or click the Paste button. Voila! The spots should disappear on the selected images.

Sync Orientation

It's important that spot removal synchronizations be used on images that have the same orientation and dimensions as the original (that is, the defects should all appear at the same image coordinates).

#24 Synchronizing Edits via Presets

If you frequently apply certain types of edits to your photos, you can create a Develop preset to apply a specific style or look to an image, or apply detailed edits. The exceptions are Spot Removal and Adjustment Brush edits; the latter is covered in Tip #29.

Here is how to create a Develop module preset:

1. Select an image from the Filmstrip that has all the Develop settings you wish to include in the preset.

2. Click the Plus (+) icon on the Presets panel, ▶ Presets ─────── +. This opens the panel and the New Develop Preset dialog box (**Figure 24a**).

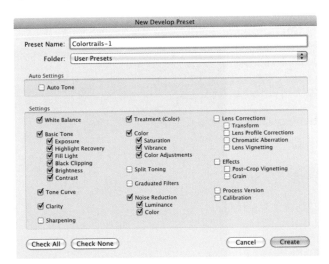

Figure 24a The New Develop Preset dialog box offers many of the same options as Copy and Paste.

3. From the dialog box, select all the Develop module settings that should be applied to many other pictures in your collection. Give the preset a name and click Create.

4. Open the Library module and select all the shots you want to sync up.

5. Open the Quick Develop panel, and from the Saved Preset pop-up menu, choose your custom preset. All edits will be applied, and you should see the changes reflected in the thumbnails (**Figure 24b**).

Figure 24b Develop presets allow you to rapidly apply and preview a custom selection of Develop settings to a large series of images directly from the Library module.

Develop Settings Context Menu

You can also right-click any of the selected photos and choose your preset from the Develop Settings submenu.

#25 Setting a Strong Foundation with Basic Edits

The Basic panel (**Figure 25a**) enables photographers to set a foundation for the global contrast and color in their photos.

Figure 25a The Basic panel (located in the Develop module) is a good place to start perfecting the tones and colors in your photos.

1. Set the white balance using the Temp slider with the mindset of how you remember the scene. Slightly Cooler? Warmer? Correct the Tint if there is a noticeable shift toward reddish or greenish hues.

2. Under the Tone controls, click Auto to set the global contrast (**Figure 25b**).

Figure 25b Start Basic edits with White Balance and Auto tone.

3. Use the Exposure slider to brighten or darken all the tones for the photo other than the brightest (Recovery) and darkest tones (Blacks). You might find that reducing Brightness and then using the Exposure slider to set the scene's general brightness value will yield good results.

4. Once you have balanced the scene's overall exposure, use the Recovery slider to restore highlight details that have been clipped. Use the Blacks slider to control where shadow details turn pure black.

5. Use Fill Light to brighten midtone areas that are still too dark; this can have a positive impact on the overall contrast of a scene (**Figure 25c**).

Figure 25c Fill Light operates on the same principle as a camera's fill flash.

(continued on next page)

Improved Fill Light

The Fill Light setting in Lightroom 3 and ACR 6 is improved and is part of the new Process 2010 versioning system described in Tip #18.

Undo: Lightroom vs. ACR

As you work through this chapter and the next, it's important to remember that Lightroom handles history in a more flexible way than ACR does. Lightroom has a History panel and can handle multiple undos quite easily. Command-Z (Mac OS) and Control-Z (Windows) will move you back through history. Command-Shift-Z (Mac OS) and Control-Shift-Z (Windows) will move you forward through the history steps. By default, ACR offers only one level of undo, but you can use the shortcuts Command-Alt-Z (Mac OS) and Control-Alt-Z (Windows) to enable multiple undos. ACR does not have a History panel.

6. If the photo is still lacking punch or contrast after using the previous settings, a modest boost to the Contrast slider can provide the desired result.

7. Increase the Clarity value for landscapes and other shots that display a lot of texture and detail; decrease the value for portraits and other shots where you desire to smooth rather than sharpen the details.

8. If the colors in your image lack presence, you may need to increase their intensity using two possible methods:

Vibrance—Reduces or boosts the colors in subtle areas (like skin tones) without clipping them.

Saturation—Works more like traditional Photoshop saturation controls, producing a more pronounced effect.

I've found that in most cases, a Vibrance setting somewhere between 15 and 40 and a Saturation setting between 0 and 10 usually provide more than enough *color punch*. Ultimately, you will want to experiment with different combinations of these two settings to achieve results that suit your tastes. **Figure 25d** shows the final shot after some basic edits.

Figure 25d Some images greatly benefit from manual control of Basic settings.

#26 Using Custom Point Curves

The most precise way to define the tones and contrast in your image is to use curves. However, between Lightroom and ACR, only the former has the ability to combine standard point curve adjustments with the Targeted Adjustment tool. Try the following steps:

1. Open the Tone Curve panel and select the Point Curve mode by clicking the Point Curve button (**Figure 26a**).

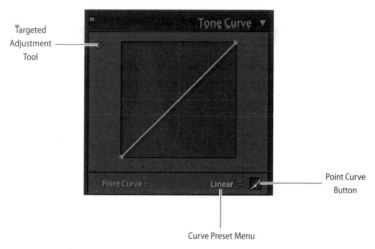

Figure 26a When working with the Tone Curve, use the Point Curve mode and set the curves preset pop-up menu to Linear to ensure a clean slate.

2. Set the curve preset to Linear using the pop-up menu. This provides a "clean slate" to begin the curve corrections.

3. Activate the Targeted Adjustment tool by clicking the small icon near the top-left portion of the Curve preview area.

4. Set points along the Tone Curve and make adjustments by clicking and dragging on the shadows, midtones, and highlights in your image. Dragging upward will brighten those tonal regions; dragging downward will darken them.

(continued on next page)

Figure 26b shows an image after creating a custom point curve.

Figure 26b Creating a custom point curve with the Targeted Adjustment tool can quickly improve on the default curve that Lightroom uses.

#27 Using Panel Previews

Lightroom allows you to preview each panel's corrections individually, or in combination by clicking the individual preview sliders, located on the left edge of each Develop panel, ▣.

By default, all Develop settings are turned on and the Basic settings are always previewed. **Figure 27a** shows all panel settings active, including the Adjustment Brush, Tone Curve, HSL, and Detail panels. **Figure 27b** shows the image with only Basic and Tone Curve edits applied.

Figure 27a All edits are active and previewed.

Figure 27b Only the Basic panel edits and Tone Curve edits are active and previewed.

#28 Perfecting Color with HSL

The Hue, Saturation, and Luminance (or HSL) controls in Lightroom and ACR are to color edits what the Basic panel and Curves panel are to tone and contrast. Photographers often face situations where one or more colors are not quite right. Maybe the skies are not a deep enough blue, maybe the grass in the field needs to be more golden, or maybe the dress on the model needs to be a darker red. These tasks can be handled with HSL.

For the scene shown in **Figure 28a**, the most important changes were to make the lower portion of the cloud formations a more vibrant orange-yellow color (less pink), and to create darker blue hues above.

Targeted HSL in ACR

HSL works the same way in ACR as it does in Lightroom. The difference is where the tools are located. After you've opened the HSL panel in ACR, the Targeted Adjustment tool in ACR will automatically mirror the HSL "mode" you choose to work with (that is, Hue, Saturation, or Luminance).

Targeted HSL

The best part about HSL is that you don't need to manually drag the sliders or use guesswork; HSL provides a Targeted Adjustment tool to define the hue, saturation, or luminance of a color region.

Figure 28a HSL can be used to recapture the "color vibe" of the original scene. This example shows clouds that have slightly washed-out colors.

Here are the steps I followed for improving the colors in this shot:

1. Open the HSL panel, then click Hue, Saturation, or Luminance to begin working in that mode.

2. Click the Targeted Adjustment tool icon and move the cursor over the color you're targeting, then drag upward to increase the color value, downward to decrease it.

3. Using the Hue mode, I dragged upward on the pinkish-orange clouds, until they looked mostly orange. This moved the yellow and orange sliders, because there are elements of both colors in the cloud.

4. Using the Saturation mode, I dragged upward again on the same orange cloud region to make the colors more vibrant in this area to approximate sunset colors. I also dragged upward slightly on the darkest blue areas to create stronger color contrast.

5. Using Luminance mode, I clicked on the side of the round building and dragged downward; this had the effect of darkening all areas that contained significant amounts of blue hue (**Figure 28b**).

Figure 28b After a few minor adjustments with HSL's Targeted Adjustment tool, the image conveyed the scene more accurately and with more drama.

#29 Creating Localized Edits: Adjustment Brush

When using Lightroom or ACR, one of the minor limitations of the applications is that nearly all the tools and adjustments create global or partially global changes. Even when you leverage the power of the HSL panel, as in the example in Tip #28, the color values often change across the image. The notable exception to this limitation is the Adjustment Brush (and the Graduated Filter tool) located in the tool strip under the Histogram panel.

Click the Adjustment Brush icon, , to pop open the Adjustment Brush settings, or press the K key. You'll notice many settings from the Basic panel are available, plus Sharpness and Color controls. This may not seem noteworthy until you consider that you can actually "paint" these settings into localized regions of your photos.

Figure 29a shows a pleasant scene, but it would look better if the water had a cooler, more inviting look. To do this, you could use other tools like HSL, but editing the blue hues in the pool would also have a pronounced impact on the sky.

Figure 29a Poolside scene in need of Lightroom's Adjustment Brush tool.

1. Modify the default settings for the Adjustment Brush so that you see where your brushstrokes are being placed (**Figure 29b**). Once the strokes are applied, you can go back and modify the settings later.

Figure 29b Initial Adjustment Brush settings can be set before you start brushwork. If the settings are set to zero, you will not be able to see the boundary of your correction.

2. Set the brush Size, Feather, and Flow rate as well as the Density (or Opacity). Here, I used a Size of 10, Feather value of 85, and Flow and Density rates of 100 (**Figure 29c**). For more subtle tasks, reduce Flow and Density so that the boundary of brushed and unbrushed areas is blurred a little more.

Figure 29c The Adjustment Brush cursor allows for a high degree of control with Size, Feather, Flow, and Density settings.

(continued on next page)

3. Click and slowly paint along the boundary of the areas you want to adjust, taking care to make sure the inner circle on the Brush cursor does not overlap areas you do not wish to change. Here, I brushed over the entire pool area, with the intent of fine-tuning the edit region (Step 4).

When you first make the brushstroke, a small circular icon called the Edit Pin will appear where you first placed the brush cursor. When you roll the cursor over this icon, you will see a reddish preview called the Mask Overlay (**Figure 29d**). Everything not shown in red is masked (that is, it won't be altered).

Figure 29d The Mask Overlay shows you which parts of your image are affected by the Adjustment settings (areas marked in red).

4. If parts of the adjustment preview overlap areas that should not change, click Erase. This activates the Erase brush, which has separate controls for Size, Feather, and Flow Rate. Press the O key to preview the adjustment area, then use the Erase brush to paint away any areas that should remain unchanged (**Figure 29e**).

Figure 29e Use the Erase brush to remove pixels from the mask.

5. Use the panel preview to gauge which settings need further adjustment. In this example, I reduced the Exposure to .21, Saturation to +7, and Clarity to –66 to smooth out the adjustment area so that it blended with the surrounding water. **Figure 29f** shows the finished result.

Figure 29f A split image of the poolside scene with Adjustment Brush settings applied (left side) and the original look of the image at right.

#30 Stylizing Black-and-White Photos with Split Toning

One of the beauties of Lightroom is that some features are less about making academic corrections and more about style. The Split Toning panel is a perfect example.

Split toning is designed to enhance or style black-and-white photos by adding subtle color effects to the highlight and shadow details. This helps to create color contrasts, add drama, or even add a sense of emotion. For example, you could split tone a winter scene to look "cool," or "icy," by adding tinges of blue.

Create a Black-and-White Photo

You need to start with a black-and-white image.

1. Select your image and click B&W in the HSL/Color/B&W panel header, HSL / Color / B&W ◀. This converts your image to grayscale values and opens the Black & White Mix controls shown in **Figure 30a**. These operate on the same principles as the HSL controls, detailed in Tip #28.

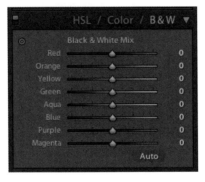

Figure 30a The Black & White Mix controls share a common panel with the HSL controls, and they can be employed in the same way by using targeted adjustments.

2. Click the Targeted Adjustment icon, then move to an area in your photo that you'd like to be lighter or darker. For this scene, I wanted the sky (background) to be darker and the flowers brighter to enhance contrast.

3. I darkened the blue skies by dragging downward on that area; this moved the Blue and Aqua sliders to the left. To brighten the flowers, I clicked one of them and dragged upward. This moved the yellow and orange sliders to the right. The resulting black-and-white picture with the settings is in **Figure 30b**.

Figure 30b The black-and-white image (prior to split toning).

Split Tone the Photo

Once your black-and-white image is ready to go, open the Split Toning panel to reveal its styling controls (**Figure 30c**). From this point, creativity takes over, and you can decide how you want to tint your images.

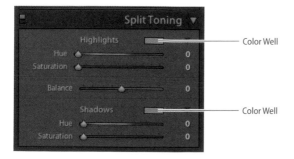

Figure 30c The Split Toning controls.

HLS Settings

As soon as you pick a color that defines both the Hue and Saturation values, you can tweak as desired.

70

ACR Split Toning

The only notable difference when split toning in ACR is that you do not have the color wells; you must choose your hue by dragging the two Hue sliders, and then choosing a Saturation value for those hues.

For this example, I wanted to keep the composition true to the original; this meant toning the flowers to be a warmer hue and toning the darker background to be a cooler hue. This also creates color contrast. To set highlight tones, click the Highlights color well to open the color ramp control (**Figure 30d**).

Figure 30d The Split Toning color controls make it easy to choose a color tint for the highlight and shadow regions in the photo.

The final step is to set a Balance between the highlight colors and shadow colors. Here, I opted to make a strong push toward highlights. The styled photo is shown in **Figure 30e**.

Figure 30e The final split-toned image with Split Toning settings shown.

#31 Creating Variations with Snapshots

As you work in Lightroom or ACR, you may reach different points in each editing session where you recognize that making further changes to a picture might result in a success or failure from an artistic or visual perspective. So how do you continue forward with your experimentation and edits without losing the look you have right now, which you like? The answer is Snapshots.

Snapshots in Lightroom are close cousins to the snapshots you create in Photoshop's History panel. The difference is that the Snapshots in Lightroom are given their own home in the user interface, rather than being grouped with the History steps (ACR also has a separate Snapshots panel, but no History panel).

Once you've reached a point in the editing process that you want to preserve, you can create a snapshot from the Snapshot panel, located in the left panel group in the Develop module. Click the Plus (+) icon, , name the snapshot, and click OK. You can continue doing this as you edit, and then click any of the snapshots in the panel (**Figure 31**) to see how they differ.

Figure 31 Snapshots are a great way to save your work as you edit each image, rather than undoing a large number of steps or starting over.

Snapshot Quick-Previewing

If you'd like to get an immediate idea of how each snapshot looks, rather than clicking and waiting a couple of seconds for it to load into the main window view, open the Navigator panel and roll the cursor over each snapshot in the list. As you do so, the Navigator preview will change on the fly.

#32 Applying Capture Sharpening

A vital part of the Lightroom workflow is to apply capture sharpening to raw files or digital negatives (DNG) before moving them into Photoshop for additional adjustments or retouching. Capture sharpening can mitigate the softening effects of anti-alias filters and other technologies found in our cameras. Lightroom 3 offers substantial improvements over the previous sharpening process.

Amount

The Amount slider controls the intensity or power of the sharpening effect. A great way to enhance your 1:1 (100% magnification) preview of the sharpening amount, is to press the Alt key as you drag the slider. This will temporarily display the image in grayscale, making it easier to detect the sharpened details. **Figure 32a** and the three screen shots that follow show a partial grayscale "overlay" so that you can see both the overlay detail and the actual image enhancement. This trick works with all the sharpening controls.

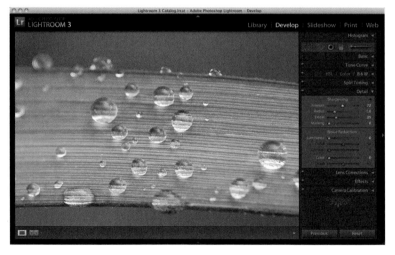

Figure 32a Press and hold the Alt key as you drag the sharpening controls and the image will temporarily display in grayscale. This makes it easier to see the degree and quality of sharpening as you modify the various settings.

Radius

The Radius slider controls the sharpening effect around hard-edged details in your photo. Lower values (less than 1.0) can provide better results for landscapes, architecture, and other shots that have a lot of small details. Here the details are shot at close range, so the setting ended up a bit higher.

As you hold down Alt and drag the slider, watch out for halos around the edges of your subject; when you don't see any obvious halos, you have reached a threshold that should enhance the detail in your image (**Figure 32b**).

Detail and Noise

If your image has plainly visible luminance or color noise, pushing the Detail slider to higher values will tend to magnify the effects of that noise.

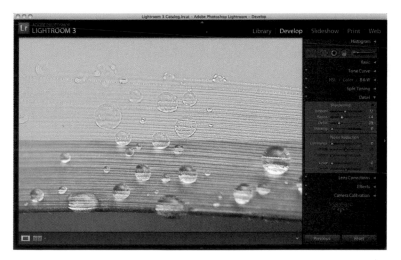

Figure 32b Pressing and holding the Alt key while moving the Radius slider can help you to control the sharpening on hard-edged details.

Detail

The Detail slider is similar to the Radius slider in its purpose, except that it controls the haloing across all details in an image (hard-edged or soft-edged). A setting of 0 is (ironically) the maximum amount of halo suppression, while a setting of 100 applies none. Typically, a setting between 25 and 50 works well for suppressing halo effects and allowing edge details to show through (**Figure 32c**).

Don't Amplify the Noise

Because sharpening can sometimes amplify luminance noise and other artifacts in your original files, it's often wise to mask areas of low detail.

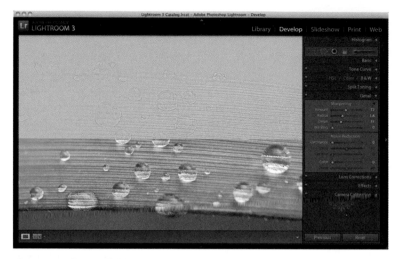

Figure 32c The Detail slider handles global halo suppression. You can also preview the image in grayscale by using the Alt key as you drag the slider.

Masking

Masking does exactly what the name implies—it masks all sharpening from specific areas of the picture. Again, press and hold the Alt key and drag the Masking slider to display a temporary preview of the masked areas. As you increase the slider value, more and more of the image will turn black. Anything that is black will not be sharpened. **Figure 32d** shows the fully masked image preview, while **Figure 32e** shows the final image with no temporary grayscale previews.

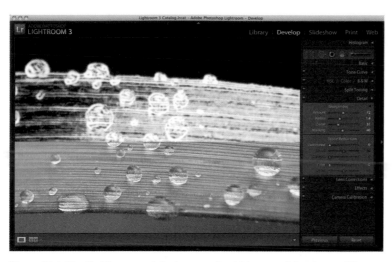

Figure 32d The Masking control displays exactly which areas of the photo will have sharpen settings applied and which will remain unsharpened (pure black areas).

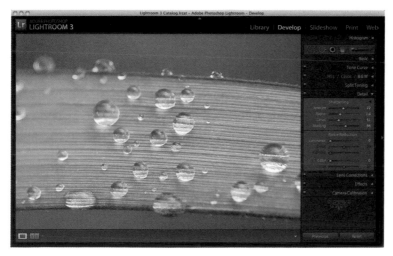

Figure 32e Lightroom 3's excellent (capture) sharpening controls make it easy to enhance the edge detail in your photographs.

Capture vs. Output Sharpening

Capture sharpening is always performed near the start of your photo-editing process in applications like Lightroom and ACR. Output sharpening is a different process that should always be handled at the end of your process, typically in Lightroom or Photoshop. That is, you sharpen output just prior to making prints.

Using ACR's Workflow Options (covered in Tip #40), or Lightroom's Print module, you can also sharpen output for computer and device screens, though the perception of that sharpening can vary depending on the individual and resolution of the screen itself.

#33 Improving Noise Reduction

Perhaps the most impressive improvement made to Lightroom 3 and ACR 6 is the improved performance of the Noise Reduction controls, specifically the Luminance Noise Reduction. Adobe's engineers have made some changes to the point where it is now possible in many cases to salvage older, high ISO files that exhibited too much noise to be used previously.

Except in situations where an image is extremely noisy in specific color regions, I have found it's no longer necessary to use third-party noise-reduction tools to achieve a clean-looking image.

The following subsections detail how the individual noise-reduction sliders work.

Luminance

Once an image has been sharpened sufficiently, make sure you're still zoomed in at 100% (or 1:1) magnification or greater and bump the Luminance slider out between 25 and 40, watching the overall graininess and noise level as you do so. You should—in many cases—be able to eliminate all or virtually all the luminance noise (**Figure 33a**).

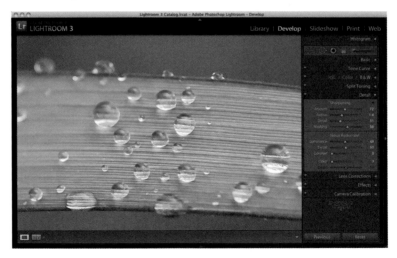

Figure 33a The sharpened photo after initial luminance noise reduction.

Detail (Luminance)

If eliminating luminance noise in your photo tends to soften the details, use the Detail slider to recover the edge contrast without reintroducing noise. Typically, I need to push this slider past a value of 50 to achieve a noticeable result (**Figure 33b**).

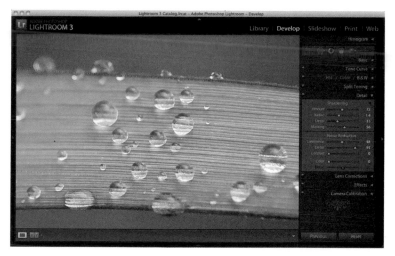

Figure 33b The Detail (Luminance) slider does a great job of recovering softened details in edge areas without reintroducing noise in others.

Contrast

For photographs that were shot with an ISO setting over 6400, you may want to try the Contrast slider to further enhance and protect the edge details that you attempted to preserve with the (Luminance) Detail slider.

Color

As the color counterpart to the Luminance slider, the Color slider removes much or all the color (or chrominance) noise in your photographs. This typically looks like splotchy mixes of green, red, and blue overlaying the detail in your image. Again, you should be able to remove most or all color noise without pushing this slider past a value of 50 (**Figure 33c**).

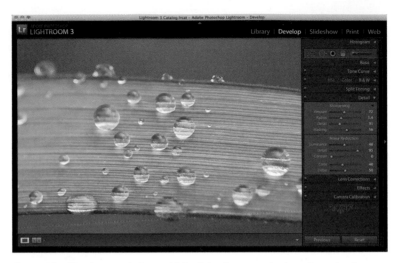

Figure 33c The sharpened photo with both luminance and color noise-reduction applied.

Detail (Color)

Similar to (Luminance) Detail, if you find that removing all the color noise from your image tends to make the edge details a little soft, you can use this slider to recover some of those lost details. Again, values over 50 seem to be the norm.

Striking a Balance

If it's not apparent yet, it's worth noting that as most of the noise in your photos is removed, beyond a certain point pushing the Luminance (or Color) slider to higher values will make the details in your photo go soft. The Sharpening and Noise Reduction controls, while making an image look cleaner, tend to work against one another when it comes to edge details.

Strike a balance and remember to keep the final screen dimensions and print dimensions of your image in mind. The smaller your final output will be, the less likely small amounts of noise will be noticed at normal viewing distances.

#34 Correcting Lens Flaws: Lens Corrections

Lightroom 3 also provides a new Lens Corrections panel that provides control over common flaws caused by the physical characteristics of lenses. Transform settings like Horizontal and Vertical distortion, Chromatic Aberration, (Barrel) Distortion, and Rotate are controllable from this new panel. To view the controls, open the Lens Corrections panel and click the Manual button (**Figure 34a**).

Figure 34a The new Lightroom Lens Corrections panel allows photographers to minimize the effects of distortions caused by their lens characteristics and other variables. Here, the Manual correction settings are shown.

Keep in mind that it's often not possible to remove 100% of the distortions that you may see in a picture because of factors that are not related to the design of the lens. For example, not only the type of lens but the lens' orientation relative to the subject can play a significant role in geometric distortion in an image.

Distortion

The Distortion slider enables you to control barrel and pincushion distortions. To counter the *barrel effect*, which causes the center of an image to bulge slightly or bow outward, drag the slider to the right until you achieve a relatively "flat-looking" appearance (**Figure 34b**). To counter the *pincushion effect*, which causes the center of an image to bow inward, drag the slider to the left until the photo appears relatively flat.

Profile Corrections

Lightroom 3 and ACR 6.1 (as well as Photoshop CS5) also offer what are called *Profile Corrections*. These fully automated corrections are generated from special profiles that characterize the way each lens bends the light that passes through it, as well as how sharp of an image it projects onto a specific camera sensor. Photoshop's Automated Lens Correction feature (part of the Lens Correction filter now) is covered in Tip #69.

Edge Work

One good way to judge an accurate correction is to find a subject in the frame that has a slightly curved edge (one that is supposed to be straight) and watch that edge as you move the Distortion slider. Find the point at which it begins to bend in the opposite direction from the original preview and then move the value back slightly until the edge is straight.

80

Empty Spaces

As you move the Distortion, Vertical, Horizontal, and Rotate sliders, you may notice gaps along the edges of your image. Two common solutions are to crop away the empty areas after you're finished or use the Scale slider to fill the gaps with an enlarged version of the image. Depending on the type of image details that are needed to fill the gaps, you can also use Content-Aware Fill in Photoshop CS5 (Tip #84).

Figure 34b Minor barrel distortions are a common occurrence and easily remedied.

Vertical

Use the Vertical slider to "untilt" a subject. If the subject appears to be falling away, slowly drag the slider to the left (**Figure 34c**). If the subject is leaning toward the viewer, drag to the right until the subject is vertical.

Figure 34c The Vertical control can help to "straighten" tall buildings.

CHAPTER TWO   Developing Raw Photos

Horizontal

If the subject of a photo appears to "shift" or fall toward the left or right side of the frame, you can use the Horizontal slider to mitigate this effect. For subjects that appear shifted toward the left side of the frame, drag the slider to the right, again paying attention to the gridlines until the image appears balanced (**Figure 34d**). For subjects that appear to shift to the right side of the frame, drag the slider to the left.

Figure 34d The Horizontal slider can lessen or remove the perception of a subject that is "shifted" away from the viewer.

Balancing Act

To get the best results, you need to balance the Vertical and Horizontal slider corrections to achieve a natural-looking perspective. Push either one too far and you're likely to create a more pronounced distraction than the one you originally intended to correct. Also, keep in mind that in many cases it may not be possible to completely remove distortions. Typically, those can be avoided only with a tilt-shift lens.

Rotate

The Rotate slider essentially performs the same function as the Straighten tool; it allows you to correct unwanted camera rotation. The primary difference is that the Rotate slider always uses the center of the original, uncropped photo as the axis point for rotating the image. Drag the slider to the left to rotate the image counterclockwise.

Scale

The Scale slider will enlarge or reduce the scale of your entire image preview, while maintaining the integrity of the corrections you have made with the other sliders. This function can be used to fill small gaps created by the other sliders. The Scale slider does not generally produce unwanted softness or artifacts; however, be aware that as you scale an image you might clip part of the subject (**Figure 34e**).

Figure 34e Use the Scale slider to fill small gaps created by the other Manual Lens Corrections settings.

Lens Vignetting

If one or more of the edges or corners in your photo need to be brightened or darkened to provide a look that is consistent with the other edges and corners, you can use the Lens Vignetting sliders.

To brighten the edges or corners of the image relative to the center, drag the Amount slider to the right, and use the Midpoint slider to define how far from the edges of the frame this correction takes effect (**Figure 34f**). Dragging the slider to the left will have the opposite effect.

Same Feature, New Name and Panel

The sliders that are currently referred to as the Lens Vignetting controls in Lightroom 3 are referred to as the Lens Correction controls in Lightroom 2, and are located in a panel called Vignettes. They perform the same function and work in exactly the same way.

Figure 34f The Lens Vignetting controls allow you to make sure there is no brightness falloff along the edges or corners of your photo. Here, the bottom-right corner of the shot has been brightened up a bit.

Chromatic Aberration

One of the minor pitfalls of using high-resolution digital cameras is that the sensors in these devices can magnify small defects in lens design. One of these defects is the inability of some lenses to focus the red, green, and blue wavelengths of light onto a specific point of the camera sensor. This results in chromatic aberration (or CA): color fringes, usually observed as a red, cyan, blue, or yellow glow along the edge of your subject.

One scenario that commonly produces CA is photographing buildings or other manmade structures that are backlit or sidelit with sunlight. It is often necessary to zoom in at 1:1 or 2:1 magnification to see CA.

If you notice a blue cast along the edge details in your image, drag the Blue/Yellow slider to the left until the cast disappears. If you notice a yellow cast, do the opposite; drag the slider to the right until the yellow cast disappears (**Figure 34g**). If you notice a cyan or reddish cast, you can follow the same process using the Red/Cyan slider.

Figure 34g Zoom in to 100% or 200% and examine the edge details of your picture to see if you can benefit from the Chromatic Aberration controls.

If, after applying the slider corrections, you still have color fringes along the edge details, choose All Edges from the Defringe pop-up menu, ![Defringe: Highlight Edges]. This may eliminate any remaining unwanted color fringes. If you see the color fringing only along very bright areas or blown-out highlights, choose Highlight Edges.

Developing Raw Photos

Figure 34h shows a before-and-after result from a Manual Lens Corrections editing session.

Figure 34h The difference before (right) and after (left) the manual mode lens corrections is obvious, even though prior to the edits the image did not at first glance appear to be badly distorted, tilted, or shifted.

#35 Going Retro: Film Grain

If you've ever had a conversation with a photographer who makes (or made) a living from black-and-white film photography, you no doubt were told of the mystical qualities of *film grain*. Unlike luminance noise from a digital camera, film grain is touted as something that can add character, grit, and emotion to a photograph. As long as the grain structure does not get in the way of the details in a composition, I believe it can add a certain character or tangible quality to the subjects.

Lightroom 3 provides new styling tools that allow you to add simulated film grain to your black-and-white (or color) photographs, in an attempt to recapture the look and feel of black-and-white film photos. You can access these by opening the new Effects panel (**Figure 35a**).

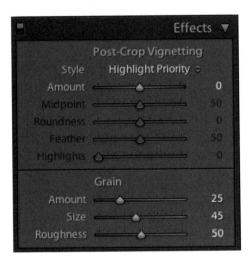

Figure 35a The new Effects panel provides controls for adding simulated film grain to black-and-white (or color) photos.

Amount

The Amount slider controls the intensity of the grain effect. So far, I have found that an amount between 25 and 40 does a solid job of mimicking the fine-grain quality of professional black-and-white films like SCALA 200x (from Agfa). **Figure 35b** shows a comparison of the same detail area with Amount settings of 25, 45, and 65, using default Size and Roughness values of 25 and 50, respectively.

Figure 35b A 1:1 (100% magnification) sample of simulated film grain, using Amounts of 25, 45, and 65 (from left to right).

Size

The Size slider controls the diameter of the individual grains that Lightroom produces. Typically, a value between 15 and 25 produces visually pleasing results (in my experience). **Figure 35c** shows grain sizes of 20, 40, and 60 over the same detail, using an Amount setting of 30.

Figure 35c A detail sample of simulated film grain using an Amount of 30, default Roughness of 50, and grain Size of 20, 40, and 60 (from left to right).

Roughness

The Roughness slider controls the smoothness of the grain effect's appearance by increasing or decreasing the local contrast around the grains. The higher the value, the rougher (or less smooth) the grain structure looks. **Figure 35d** shows the results of adjusting the Roughness settings.

Figure 35d A detail sample of simulated film grain using an Amount of 30, Size of 25, and Roughness settings of 25, 50, and 75 (from left to right).

Figure 35e shows the same photograph, zoomed out, after the Grain effect was applied. Final settings are Amount 30, Size 25, and Roughness 35.

Figure 35e Adding simulated film grain can enhance the look or mood of many black-and-white photographs (in this shooter's opinion).

#36 Prepping Files for HDR Pro

High Dynamic Range (or HDR) photographs use a series of staggered or "bracketed" exposures to create a single photograph that captures the range of tonal details (from the very brightest to the very darkest). This process is accomplished using Photoshop CS5's Merge to HDR Pro function, which is covered in detail in Chapter 4, "Perfecting Images with Photoshop CS5."

There are a few simple steps to follow when preparing your bracketed raw exposures in Lightroom for an HDR workflow. These steps will help you to get the best possible results when tone mapping the data in your images (Tip #74). Additional tips relating to the actual capture of shots destined for HDR are covered in Tip #72.

1. As a rule, you generally do not want to alter the settings related to image exposure (that is, any setting that makes your image brighter or darker, in part or whole). The point of taking multiple exposures is so Photoshop can use the best tonal components of each shot (Blacks, Fill Light, Exposure, Recovery) and merge them into a single shot. Once that's done, then it's time to handle all the exposure-related edits in Merge to HDR Pro.

2. Be sure to synchronize (using Copy and Paste—see Tip #23) any changes you make to the color character of a given image in the series. Color styling can be handled in Photoshop CS5.

   Note
   The steps for synchronizing files in ACR are in Tip #38.

3. Take advantage of the improved Capture Sharpening and Noise Reduction controls (Tips #32 and #33, respectively), again making sure to synchronize the settings (particularly the Sharpening settings, to avoid any possible ghosting issues later). Excess noise can have quite a negative impact on the tone mapping process, so it's best to eliminate as much of it as possible before the merge.

4. Check for Chromatic Aberrations (CA) and use the Lens Corrections panel to remove or minimize any that you find. CA can also have a negative impact when using Merge to HDR Pro in Photoshop CS5, because it can cause problems with precise image alignments and other processes. If you find that each image in the series has the same

Camera Hints

Before you ever take the bracketed exposure, be sure to optimize your ISO settings to minimize any potential noise issues, and use a tripod (or at the very least a lens that supports vibration reduction). A little bit of camera shake from the wind or an unsteady hand can ruin an otherwise excellent series of exposures.

CA problem, in the same part of the image, you can synchronize these edits; otherwise, they can and should be handled on a per-image basis.

5. When you're ready to move the images into Photoshop CS5, select them in the Filmstrip, right-click, and choose Edit In > Merge to HDR Pro in Photoshop (**Figure 36**).

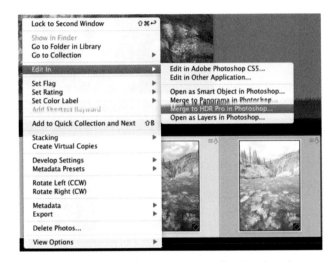

Figure 36 It's easy to send your prepped raw files directly to the Merge to HDR Pro interface from Lightroom 3.

#37 Exporting Files

Once you've finished with your edits for a particular file or series of files, you may want to save those to a new format for later use (such as PSD or TIFF files). To do this, you'll need to jump back to the Library module, select the image or images that you wish to export, and then click Export, Export . This will open the Export Files window (**Figure 37a**).

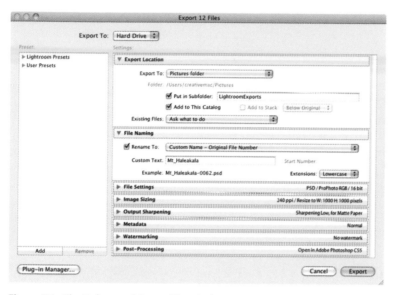

Figure 37a The Lightroom 3 Export Files window.

There are three functions that directly impact file quality: File Settings, Image Sizing, and Output Sharpening.

File Settings

File Settings are critical because they impact how the final colors and details in your image are handled on export. If you plan to work on the files in Photoshop CS5, the PSD or TIFF formats will serve you well.

To maintain the color appearance generated in Lightroom, choose ProPhoto RGB from the Color Space pop-up menu. This is Lightroom's native color space. If you need to export the files so that other parties can edit them, you can choose the Adobe RGB 1998 color space; this is a de facto standard that should be available to anyone using the Adobe Creative Suite, going back several versions.

To maintain the maximum amount of image data from your raw file, choose a Bit Depth of 16 bits. All three settings can be seen in **Figure 37b**.

Figure 37b For files that need further editing in Photoshop CS5 and that need to maintain color fidelity with your Lightroom edits, it's usually best to choose the PSD or TIFF file format, the ProPhoto RGB color space, and 16 bits/component Bit Depth options.

Image Sizing

For some situations, you may need to resize (typically reduce) your large Digital SLR (or DSLR) files when exporting them. Note that regardless of which size or resolution you choose, Lightroom 3 will automatically apply the correct algorithm Resize settings shown in **Figure 37c**.

Figure 37c Lightroom 3 export Image Sizing settings.

Output Sharpening

Finally, depending on what the finished output of your photos will be (screen or print), you have options to apply Output Sharpening to your files (**Figure 37d**).

Figure 37d Lightroom 3 export Output Sharpening settings.

#38 ACR: Synchronizing Edits

You can save yourself a lot of time by carefully applying a series of edits to one file, and then synchronizing all these same edits with other, very similar files (often shots from the same shoot). ACR accomplishes this with a Synchronize button and dialog box. There is a catch: Because ACR does not allow you to browse through image thumbnails in your folders, the synchronization process must start in Photoshop or Bridge.

1. Using the File > Open command from Photoshop, Mini Bridge, or Bridge CS5, select all the files for which you need to synchronize edits, and then open them into ACR 6.1. You can see the results in **Figure 38a**.

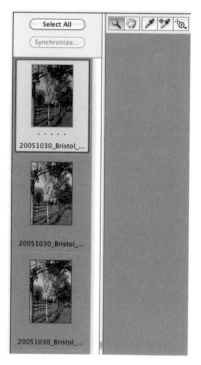

Figure 38a Multiple files opened in ACR.

2. Select one file as your baseline image, and carefully apply all the edits you wish to make, making note of which settings you change.

3. Click the Select All button near the top-left part of the ACR UI, or press Command-A (Mac OS) or Control-A (Windows). This will highlight all your remaining images in the series.

(continued on next page)

ACR-Specific Settings

As noted in the beginning of the chapter, virtually all the raw development tools and settings in Lightroom 3 and ACR 6.1 look and work in the same way. However, there are three areas in particular that are different enough in ACR to warrant their own tips so you can examine the differences in the user interfaces and steps to produce a given result.

4. Click the Synchronize button; this will open the Synchronize dialog box. Select the items that correlate to the edits you made in Step 2 (**Figure 38b**).

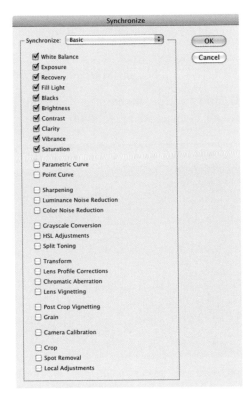

Figure 38b The ACR Synchronize dialog box works in much the same way as the Synchronize Settings dialog box in Lightroom 3.

5. When you click OK, all the settings you chose will be applied to the remaining selected images. The changes you made will become visible on the selected thumbnails; you will see the changes in terms of what the thumbnails look like, or you will see an Edits badge that denotes changes have been made to an image, .

You can use this process to synchronize things like spot removals or prepping a series of files for Merge to HDR Pro.

#39 ACR: Saving Images

When you're finished with your edits in ACR, the process of exporting files is referred to as *saving images*. As with the Synchronize feature, if you wish to save or export multiple files simultaneously, you need to open all of them ahead of the edits you make. To access ACR's file-saving options, click the Save Images button (Save Images...) . This will open a dialog box that provides simple options for choosing a Location, File Name, and Format (**Figure 39**).

To access the important settings that can affect file quality (as noted in Tip #37), you'll need to set those values in the Workflow Options (explained in Tip #40).

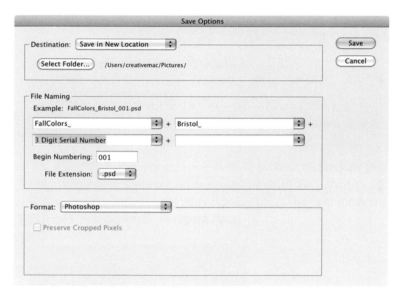

Figure 39 ACR Save Options dialog box. Note that important settings like Color Space, File Size, and Output Sharpening are all accessed from the Output Settings dialog box, covered in Tip #40.

#40 ACR: Workflow Options

To ensure that the files you save use the appropriate settings (as mentioned in Tip #37), click the blue hyperlink at the bottom-center portion of the ACR window Adobe RGB (1998); 16 bit; 2000 by 3008 (6.0MP); 240 ppi . This will open the Workflow Options dialog box that contains settings for (Color) Space, (Bit) Depth, Size, Resolution, and Output Sharpening, as seen in **Figure 40**. All the same guidelines apply as in Tip #37.

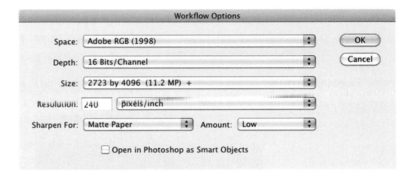

Figure 40 ACR Output Options dialog box is where you apply the various settings prior to saving your finished files to your hard drive.

CHAPTER THREE

Lightroom 3 Output Hints

Output is about providing your photographs in a medium and format that your clients or other interested parties can use right away. Whether they intend to quickly evaluate some shots before making final choices, or whether they intend to have a print framed and hung right away, the idea is to help them find the shots they need quickly and display them at a size that suits the context.

Perhaps more than the other components of a digital workflow, the output options for Lightroom 3 stand apart from those in Adobe Bridge CS5 and other applications. For this reason, this chapter focuses only on Lightroom 3 output.

However, because there are three separate output modules in Lightroom (Slideshow, Print, and Web), each with a large array of features and controls for perfecting the look of your photos, to cover each in detail is not feasible for this title. I've gathered some important tips and techniques that will (hopefully) help you get a quick start with Lightroom 3 output. If you need an A–Z reference for all of Lightroom's features, *The Adobe Photoshop Lightroom 3 Book: The Complete Guide for Photographers*, by Martin Evening, is worth a look. Its content is almost 600 pages in length, but you should find the extra time investment worthwhile.

Let's start with a new feature that isn't limited strictly to the output modules but which is closely related in purpose—watermarking. From there we'll take a look at some tips for each module, in sequence, starting with the Slideshow module.

#41 Watermark Editor

Tip

To cycle through the images you have selected while working in the Watermark Editor, click the arrow buttons at the top of the editor.

The concept of a watermark originated with hand drawings and other forms of printed art long before there was a digital camera or even the idea of one. Essentially, the concept is that you place a small "mark" on your artwork that lets people know who created the work.

For the purposes of this book, we'll use *visual watermarks*. While easy to create, the main drawback to a visual watermark is that it is often easy to remove. There are also *digital watermarks* that are available as third-party plugins. They are much more difficult to notice or remove, but they're also more complicated to set up. Using digital watermarks requires special software from companies, such as Digimarc, as well as a subscription.

To use watermarks in Lightroom 3, select your image(s), then choose Lightroom > Edit Watermarks (Mac OS) or Edit > Edit Watermarks (Windows) from the main menu (**Figure 41a**).

Figure 41a The new Lightroom 3 Watermark Editor.

Applying a Graphic Watermark

If you prefer to use your company logo or other graphic as your water-mark, you need to save that logo as a JPEG or PNG file before applying it to your photo in Lightroom 3. If your logo or graphic uses transparency, you'll want to save to the PNG format because it supports transparency options. When you're ready to bring your graphic into the Watermark Editor, choose Graphic as the Watermark Style, navigate to your hard drive to locate the graphic file, and add it to the photo (**Figure 41b**).

Figure 41b You can add a logo or other graphical watermark to your photos with Lightroom 3; just be sure to save a version in JPEG or PNG format first.

Digimarc and Photoshop

Since 1996, each version of Adobe Photoshop and Adobe Photoshop Elements has shipped with a Digimarc demo plug-in, found in the Filters menu. Although it does not allow you to apply a unique digital ID to each shot, the plug-in does allow you to experiment with digital watermarking until you're ready to purchase a unique ID (via subscription to the Digimarc service). You can learn more at Digimarc.com.

Once the graphic is visible in the Watermark Editor's preview area, use the Watermark Effects controls to define its opacity, scale, position, and rotation (**Figure 41c**). These same controls work on text watermarks.

Figure 41c The Watermark Effects controls allow you to modify the appearance and location of your graphic.

The Inset controls define how the graphic will be placed, using a chosen corner or edge of the photo. That corner or edge, in turn, is defined by the Anchor control. Figure 41c shows the logo anchored to the bottom-right of the image with modified Inset values.

Applying a Text Watermark

Choose Text as the Watermark Style and type your watermark words or symbols in the text box at the bottom of the editor window. The Text Options and Watermark Effects controls format your text (**Figure 41d**).

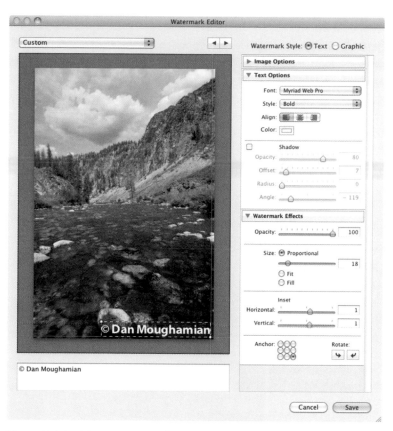

Figure 41d Applying text watermarks in Lightroom 3 is a snap using the Watermark Editor's text field and text controls.

By default, a drop shadow will be added to your text watermark. There are four settings that control the look of drop shadows:

- **Opacity**—Controls how light or dark the shadow is

- **Offset**—Controls the distance the shadow falls from the text

- **Radius**—Controls how soft or hard the shadow edge is

- **Angle**—Controls the angle the simulated light source

You can insert a few special symbols using some keyboard key combinations. The first three use Mac OS keyboard conventions, the final three use Windows conventions. These should work on most western keyboard systems.

- Copyright symbol© (Mac): Press and hold the Alt key and type G.

- Trademark symbol™ (Mac): Press and hold Alt and type 2.

- Registered symbol® (Mac): Press and hold Alt and type R.

- Copyright symbol© (Windows): Press and hold the Alt key and use the numeric keypad to type 0169 (make sure your Number Lock key is on).

- Trademark symbol™ (Windows): Press and hold the Alt key and use the numeric keypad to type 0153.

- Registered symbol® (Windows): Press and hold the Alt key and use the numeric keyboard to type 0174.

The results of using a text Shadow are shown in **Figure 41e**.

Figure 41e Drop shadows are easily applied to text watermarks in the Watermark Editor.

Using Watermark Presets

To reuse a specific logo or text watermark on multiple images, click the pop-up menu at the top of the Watermark Editor, and choose Save Current Settings as New Preset (**Figure 41f**). You can use the same pop-up menu to delete or rename a preset.

Figure 41f Use the pop-up menu in the Watermark Editor to save your customized watermark as a preset.

If you need to modify an existing preset, choose it from the pop-up menu, change your settings, and choose Update Preset (**Figure 41g**).

Figure 41g The pop-up can also be used to delete, rename, and update existing presets.

#42 Polishing Slideshow Layouts

Slideshows can be one of the most effective (and fun) ways to impress a client. For this tip we'll take the default Lightroom slideshow layout and make some important tweaks so that it has more of a custom look. The key thing to remember with slideshows is that although it's possible to add all sorts of graphical extras and effects, ultimately the show is about the pictures, not the background that accompanies them. Less is often more.

Slideshow Setup

The first step is to make sure that you have an assortment of photos to populate the slideshow. You can accomplish this in several ways.

- Select a range of images in the Library module's Grid view and then open the Slideshow module. The images appear in the Filmstrip.

- Create a collection of photos and open the Slideshow module. Open the Collections panel and choose your collection. The images appear in the Filmstrip.

- Go directly to the Slideshow module without any images selected (or collected), use the Filmstrip to select a group of images.

I prefer the second method, because any type of collection is an easier entity to maintain and modify than a temporary selection of photos. Next, make sure the Default option is selected from the Template Browser (**Figure 42a**).

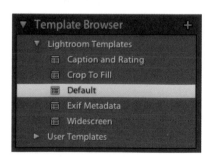

Figure 42a Once a selection of images or an image Collection is active in the Slideshow module, starting with the Default template provides a "clean slate" for creating slideshows.

Slideshow Options

To begin customizing the slideshow layout, open the Options panel and deselect Zoom to Fill Frame. Leaving this option selected will cause the entire frame of the slideshow to be filled by enlarging each image preview to fit. This often causes unwanted cropping and is especially true of shots that use a portrait orientation.

Next, click the Stroke Border option, choose a width somewhere between 2 and 5 pixels, and change the color of the stroke to a light gray or white. This will contrast nicely with the dark background in the Default template. Finally, deselect Cast Shadow, because it will be difficult if not impossible to see a drop shadow against a dark background. The results are shown in **Figure 42b**.

Figure 42b Slideshow options allow you to ensure that your photos will not be cropped unnecessarily and to create points of contrast between the photo and the background.

Slideshow Layout

The Layout panel in the Slideshow module only controls the margins. All that's needed is to move one of the sliders to the left to decrease the margin value a bit, so you can use more of the available space. Because the values are linked by default, moving one slider will move all of them an equal amount. To unlink them, turn off the Link All widget, Link All. The layout results are shown in **Figure 42c**.

Figure 42c The Slideshow's layout controls only modify the margin values.

Slideshow Overlays

The Overlays panel controls several visual effects and bits of information that you can include with each slide during playback.

1. Deselect the Identity Plate option.

The Identity Plate is a feature that allows you to add a watermark-like emblem or text string to your slideshow. The main differences between identity plates and watermarks is that identity plates sit atop the empty space in the slideshow (not the photo itself) and are anchored automatically to the top-left part of the canvas. However, because there is limited control over identity-plate appearance and placement, I use watermarks when I want viewers to see my copyright or company name.

2. Click the Watermarking option to activate the watermark. You can use the pop-up menu to choose custom presets (see Tip #41).

3. Turn off Ratings Stars and Text Overlays. Unless a client asks to see specific information with the images, adding extraneous visual input to a slideshow will distract from the photographs. Settings for the Overlays panel are shown in **Figure 42d**.

(continued on next page)

Choosing Colors

Throughout the book, you will notice references to *"color boxes" or "color wells."* These are essentially small squares or rectangles that display a solid color, and when you click them, you open one of Adobe's color pickers. Each will be different depending on the application you're using, but all serve the same purpose: to provide a means of choosing a color for the designated effect or style.

Figure 42d Limiting the "visual extras" to just a simple watermark (or an identity plate if you prefer) can help to keep viewers focused on the photographs.

Slideshow Backdrop

The Backdrop panel (**Figure 42e**) allows you to create different kinds of visual contrast between your photograph (the foreground) and the background.

Figure 42e The Backdrop panel provides useful tools for creating contrast between the photograph and the background. The Color Wash creates a subtle gradient effect.

1. Make sure both the background image and background color options are deselected, and make sure the Color Wash option is selected.

   Color wash creates a gradient backdrop for your photograph, which can add a touch of style to the presentation without distracting from the photo. The easiest way to see this is by clicking the color box or color well (directly opposite the Color Wash option) and selecting a light shade of gray using the Eyedropper tool.

2. If you'd like to add a subtle hue to the gradient, drag the saturation slider (located above the word "HEX") upward slightly to view a color ramp, and again choose your hue and tone value with the Eyedropper tool (**Figure 42f**). Here a faint blue-violet tone was chosen to add a subtle color accent.

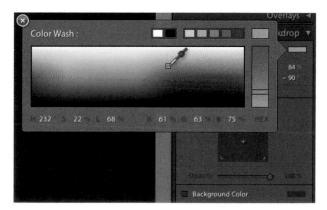

Figure 42f The Color Wash option allows you to choose a shade of gray or a color tint to customize the look of the gradient backdrop.

3. Use the Angle controls to set the angle of the gradient. To create a subtle top-down gradient with your chosen shade or tint on the bottom, set this value to –90.

4. Use the Opacity slider to fade the gradient out, mixing with the default background of black. The final gradient is shown in **Figure 42g**.

(continued on next page)

Colors Can Distract

Generally, it's wise to avoid using a saturated color, because having areas of intense color near a photo can change the perception of that photo's colors.

Figure 42g Gradient backdrops can create an added element of style and contrast.

Slideshow Titles

To create an intro screen and ending screen, select the Intro Screen and End Screen options. This will activate the Identity Plate controls in the panel (**Figure 42h**).

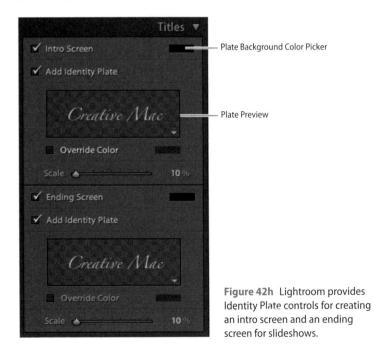

Figure 42h Lightroom provides Identity Plate controls for creating an intro screen and an ending screen for slideshows.

You can edit either of the identity plates with a few steps.

1. Click and hold the small triangle shown in the Identity Plate preview, and choose Edit from the pop-up menu. This opens the Identity Plate Editor (**Figure 42i**). Like the Watermark Editor discussed earlier in the chapter, the Identity Plate Editor defines whether the plate uses text or graphics. The editor provides basic font controls like Font Face, Size, and Color (**Figure 42j**). If the text is cut off, you can extend the size of the dialog box.

Caution

Select or delete the default text before changing font settings.

Figure 42i The default identity plate can be customized by choosing Edit from the Identity Plate Preview's pop-up menu.

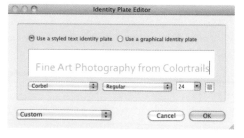

Figure 42j The Identity Plate Editor allows you to create text plates directly or add graphical plates from your hard drive.

2. To save a new plate as a preset, use the Custom pop-up menu shown in Figure 42j, choose Save As, and give the plate a name.

3. Click OK to add the new plate to the slideshow and preview it.

4. Drag the Scale slider to the right to increase the text size (**Figure 42k**).

(continued on next page)

Figure 42k Custom Identity Plates are easily created for intros and endings.

5. To change the color of the intro or ending text without reopening the Identity Plate Editor, click the Override Color option, Override Color .

6. Click the color box to preview the plate and select a new color (**Figure 42l**).

Figure 42l The color of the identity plate text in the intro or ending can be overridden using the Override Color control.

#43 Slide Duration and Transitions

The Playback panel provides a number of options for further customizing slideshows, including a simple control that lets you pick a music file from your hard drive to act as a soundtrack, as well as options for displaying photos in random order and whether to repeat a finished show. However, the most important playback options (and ones that also affect the look of the slideshow) are the Slide Duration controls (**Figure 43**).

Figure 43 Slide Duration controls let you quickly set the length of time each slide displays (including transition duration), as well as the option to set a color as part of the standard transition.

Slides control—Defines in seconds how long each photograph displays in full (without the transition between photos being taken into consideration).

Fades control—Defines in seconds how long it will take for one photo to "blend" into the next as part of the transition.

Color option—Defines the background color shown at the midpoint in each slide transition.

#44 Exporting Slideshows as Video

New to Lightroom 3 is the ability to create a self-contained video file from a slideshow, enabling you to easily share slideshows online and elsewhere. Once a slideshow has been customized and tested via play-back, export the show by clicking the Export Video button at the bottom portion of the left panel group.

This will open a system dialog box that has a single pop-up menu for choosing the size of the video, called Video Preset. As you choose each size option, a description of its purpose displays below the pop-up menu (**Figure 44**). To export, choose a file name, save location and video resolution, then click Export to create MP4 files that you can embed into websites or burn to DVD.

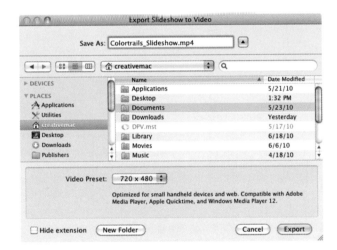

Figure 44 Exporting slideshows from Lightroom 3 is a very simple and intuitive process.

#45 Quick Contact Sheets

Lightroom 3's Contact Sheet feature is located in the Print module. As with the slideshow, the setup for creating a contact sheet is simple:

1. Create a collection of photos for your sheet. When you select those images from the Collections panel in the Print module, they will appear in the Filmstrip. As with slideshows, you can also use manual selections from the Library module, or use the Filmstrip and its pop-up menu in the Print module, similar to the steps described in Tip #42. Open the Print module.

2. Make sure the Single Image/Contact Sheet option is selected in the Layout Style panel (it should be active by default),

3. Open the Template Browser panel and choose 4×5 Contact Sheet or 5×8 Contact Sheet as a starting point. The template names refer to the number of columns and rows to be printed on a single sheet of paper.

Layout Panel

The Layout panel provides options for ensuring that all the thumbnails or "cells" in the contact sheet are sized and spaced in a way that makes maximum use of the paper size, while also ensuring the thumbnails will be large enough to evaluate after printing (**Figure 45a**).

Figure 45a The Layout panel is a good place to start when customizing a contact sheet.

Margins—Use these controls to define the amount of space that is left between the edge of the paper and the outer edges of the thumbnails. Leave these at the default settings if you want to maximize the available space.

Page Grid—Use these two sliders to control the number of rows and columns that will be printed. The more rows and columns, the smaller each printed thumbnail will be. I generally find a 4×4 arrangement (16 photos) to be a good compromise between quantity of images and thumbnail size.

Cell Spacing—Use these controls to determine the amount of empty space left between thumbnail cells. These work in tandem with the Cell Size sliders; changing either set of values will impact the other. If turned on, try deselecting the Keep Square option under Cell Size and setting a Cell Spacing value around .20 inches. This should maximize the size of portrait-oriented photos while maintaining visual spacing between thumbnails.

Page Panel

The Page panel provides a range of options to define the page marks, colors, and information that will be printed along with your thumbnails. These options include Page Background Color, Identity Plate, Watermarking, Page Numbering, Page Info, Crop Marks, and Photo Info (**Figure 45b**).

Figure 45b The Page panel allows you to apply copyright and other useful information to the contact sheet.

To use the Photo Info option, click the Photo Info check box and choose a type of information from the pop-up menu. In this example, Exposure info has been chosen and is reflected underneath each photo. You can also tweak the font size.

Print Job Panel

Once a contact sheet is ready to print, the Print Job panel is the final stop before defining your Page Setup options and Print Settings. The first thing you may want to do is turn off the Draft Mode Printing option. This will enable you to set options for Print Resolution, Print Sharpening, Media Type, Bit Depth, and Color Management options (**Figure 45c**).

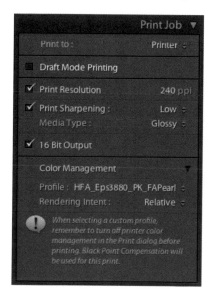

Figure 45c The Print Job panel offers several options for optimizing your print quality.

Print Resolution—This should default to the native resolution of your images. For example, the native resolution of all my Nikon DSLRs is 240ppi (pixels per inch). For the most part, you should leave the default setting intact unless you have special instructions from your printer manual or other source to change it to a more optimal setting based on the printer itself.

Print Sharpening—This applies extra sharpening at the end of any digital photography workflow to enhance the local contrast in printed output. A setting of Low or Standard should suffice for most images.

Printer Settings

When using a custom-color profile, be sure to turn off the color-management option in your printer driver software.

If you still cannot achieve crisp-looking output at those settings, you may want to reevaluate the Capture Sharpening settings in the Detail panel, as well as the amount of Luminance Noise reduction. These can play a role in print sharpness.

Media Type—This setting defines whether you're printing to a matte-based paper or glossy paper. For "in-between" types like pearl or semi-gloss finishes, choose the Glossy option.

16-bit Output—This setting helps to maintain subtle color and tonal details when printing raw files or DNG files. Although you may not always notice a difference, there is no harm in leaving this selected for images greater than 8 bits, assuming your printer supports 16-bit data. For JPEG images, you can safely leave this deselected and not suffer any quality setbacks. Note that choosing this option will tend to slow your print times a bit.

Color Management—This setting allows you to set a color profile and rendering intent, as provided by your printer's driver. Choose a profile that is specific not only to your printer, but to the paper you are using (these can often be downloaded from the paper manufacturer's websites).

Rendering Intent—This setting allows you to choose the Perceptual or Relative (Colorimetric) rendering style. The default (Perceptual) will normally produce pleasing results for most images. If you find slightly perceptible color shifts or other anomalies, try the Relative option and compare the two printed results.

#46 Custom Photo Packages

Photo Packages are a convenient way for photographers to create multiple prints of differing size on a single sheet of paper. To create a customized print package, again choose your collection of images and click Custom Package from the Layout Style panel.

Starting with an empty canvas (**Figure 46a**) will provide the most options. So if the canvas is not empty, click any of the boxes to select and highlight them, then press the Delete key to remove them.

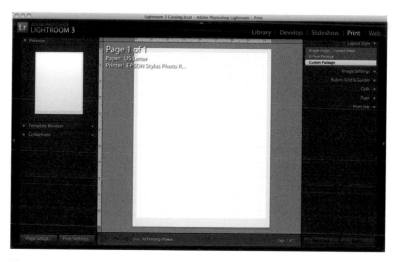

Figure 46a Start your custom photo package with an empty canvas to give yourself as many options as possible as you start to add cells.

Rulers, Grid & Guides Panel

In order to quickly set up a custom layout for a photo package, open the Rulers, Grid & Guides panel and make sure the Grid Snap option is set to Grid. This will ensure that as the image cells are moved, they will snap to the nearest gridline, making alignment much quicker. The settings for this panel are shown in **Figure 46b**.

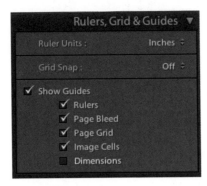

Figure 46b Guides and grid snapping can help to quickly lay out a custom photo package.

Cells Panel

The Cells panel is where the majority of the customization and work gets done when creating custom photo packages. You can think of cells as the placeholders for an image. The Cells panel provides several controls for adding picture cells of different sizes to the canvas.

1. Add four or five default-size image cells by clicking the buttons that match the sizes you want to use (**Figure 46c**).

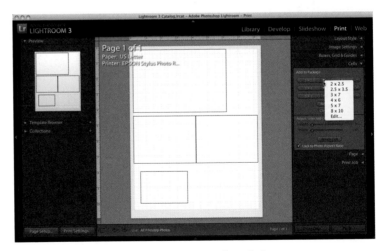

Figure 46c Click the cell buttons to add new cells to the layout.

Notice each cell button has two segments (highlighted in beige here to delineate each—these colors are not present in Lightroom). Click the left side of each cell button to add a cell of that size, , or click the right side to choose a new size or define a custom size, .

After adding the first few cells, adjust their orientation and position before adding more. If you try to add more cells than the sheet can hold at their default orientation and positions, Lightroom will add a new page to your custom Photo Package (more on this shortly).

2. Rotate a cell by clicking it once to highlight it and then clicking the Rotate Cell button, . This will rotate the cell by 180 degrees.

3. Move a cell by dragging it to a desired location; use the grid to help you align cell edges **(Figure 46d)**.

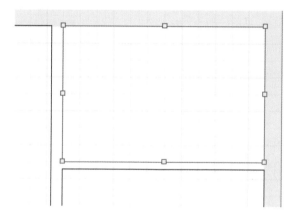

Figure 46d Rotate and move image cells to maximize available layout space.

4. Resize a cell by selecting it, pressing and holding the Shift key (this will maintain its proportions), then dragging a corner of the cell to resize it **(Figure 46e)**. This can be helpful if there is a tight fit between cells and the edge of the page.

(continued on next page)

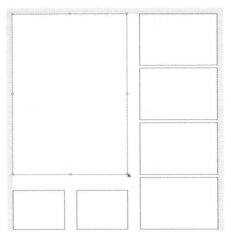

Figure 46e Resize image cells while maintaining their proportions in order to create alignment and space between cells, so that the finished package prints can be trimmed without cutting away parts of the photos.

5. To add an additional page and begin a new custom layout by clicking the New Page button, [New Page].

A new page will appear next to the original (**Figure 46f**).

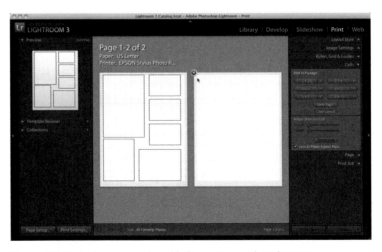

Figure 46f Multiple pages can be added to custom package layouts.

Remember that what the printed package sheet ultimately looks like is not really important. What matters most is how efficiently the custom layout allows you to trim the prints, without wasting paper.

Pay attention to the edges of your photos; line them up whenever possible. **Figure 46g** shows a custom layout with several cell edges aligned and the page orientation set to Landscape using the Page Setup button, Page Setup... , located at the bottom of the left panel group.

6. Click the Clear Layout button, Clear Layout , to start over. Sometimes Lightroom will add an extra page when the last cell you added is just slightly too large to fit. If that happens, you can drag the new cell over to the original page and click the red ✕, , on the new page to delete it.

7. The final step is to drop the actual photographs in their respective cells. To do this, simply drag them one at a time from the Filmstrip into the cell (**Figure 46g**).

Remember to match the orientation of the photos to the orientation of the cells so that you do not crop the photos or cause unwanted cell rotation. Lightroom will crop and rotate photos automatically to fit ones whose orientation does not match the cell in which you place it.

Figure 46g Populate image cells by dragging and dropping individual photos directly from the Filmstrip.

#47 Airtight Web Galleries

Lightroom's Web module comes with three types of Web galleries that can be built for a collection of photos: Airtight Interactive galleries, Flash galleries, and HTML galleries. This tip will briefly cover the three types of Airtight Interactive galleries, which use a combination of HTML and JavaScript to add extra design flair and interactivity to a gallery.

To set up any of the Web galleries, open the Web module, click the type of gallery you wish to create from the Layout Style panel, and choose a Collection of photos from the Collections panel.

Airtight AutoViewer

The Airtight AutoViewer gallery template creates a web page where your photos scroll across your page (either via automatic playback or manual clicks), without actually requiring the browser's scroll bar. You can think of the page background as a "stage" that houses a continuous filmstrip-like presentation of your photos. As you click, a new photo enters from the right and disappears on the left as you click and view new photos (**Figure 47a**).

Figure 47a The Airtight AutoViewer gallery uses HTML and JavaScript to create a simulated "stage" where a filmstrip-like presentation moves across the screen.

Formatting options for the Airtight AutoViewer gallery allow you to customize background and border colors; adjust padding between images; apply label information; modify dimensions (long edge) and (JPEG) quality; and determine whether to apply watermarks or screen sharpening to the photos (**Figure 47b**).

Figure 47b Formatting options for the Airtight AutoViewer gallery are relatively sparse and simple, focusing mostly on borders and padding options.

Airtight PostcardViewer

The Airtight PostcardViewer gallery template also uses scripting tricks to create a stack of simulated "postcards" that are laid out on the web page, much like slides are laid out on a lightbox (**Figure 47c**).

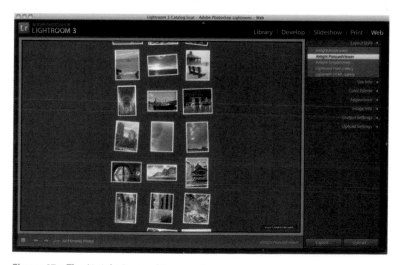

Figure 47c The Airtight PostcardViewer gallery.

Just click a photo and the viewer will zoom in on that photo (**Figure 47d**). Click the thumbnail again or on an empty space to return.

Figure 47d To "zoom in" on a photo in an Airtight PostcardViewer gallery, click an image; to zoom back out, click the image a second time or click an empty area.

When formatting an Airtight PostcardViewer gallery, use the Appearance panel to set the number of image columns, as well as to control the size of the thumbnails and zoomed-in photos (**Figure 47e**).

Figure 47e Use the Airtight PostcardViewer's Appearance panel to ensure as many thumbnails as possible are visible on the page.

As with the Airtight AutoViewer gallery, you can use the Image Info and Output Settings panel to apply information, such as captions and settings, image size (long edge), and (JPEG) quality.

Airtight SimpleViewer

The Airtight SimpleViewer gallery template looks more like a traditional HTML gallery format, with a grid of small thumbnails placed next to a large preview of the current (or active) photo. Simply click any thumbnail to get a larger preview of that image. The main advantage is that this template uses a very small space to convey a relatively large amount of information about your photos (**Figure 47f**).

Figure 47f The SimpleViewer looks like a traditional HTML gallery, using a combination of thumbnails and a single large preview to view photographs.

The formatting options for customizing the Airtight SimpleViewer gallery layout are similar to those used with the other Airtight galleries. The main concern is to ensure your large preview is large enough to help people evaluate the image, and to define the number of thumbnails (by controlling the number of rows and columns in the Appearance panel) so that the "stage" content is visually balanced (**Figure 47g**). Tweaking the Photo Borders and Padding settings can also help to line things up a bit.

Uploading

For all the Web module galleries, you need to supply your own FTP or login information (via the Upload Settings panel) in order to have Lightroom 3 move the files from your local drive to your server location. Use the FTP Server pop-up menu to open the Configure FTP dialog box,

Figure 47g The Airtight SimpleViewer gallery's most important formatting controls are the Size, Photo Borders, and Padding settings (Output Settings panel), and the Stage options (Appearance panel). These help to balance the look of the page.

#**48** Lightroom Flash Gallery

For those not familiar with Flash, it is an Adobe technology designed to add rich media and interactivity to the web and web applications. This makes it a natural fit for photo galleries. To get started with Flash galleries in Lightroom, click the Lightroom Flash Gallery option in the Layout Style panel. This opens the Flash Gallery (default) web template in the Templates panel. The default template uses a filmstrip-style layout that includes a scrolling thumbnail list, a large preview area, a page header, and simple controls for viewing photos (**Figure 48a**).

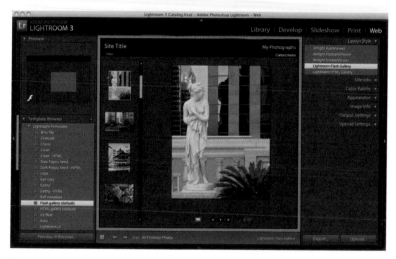

Figure 48a The default Flash Gallery template provides a simple filmstrip-and-preview design that you can customize to display the look you want.

There are additional Flash templates that you can access from the Template Browser panel. Make sure the Preview panel is also open and roll the cursor over each template's name in the browser to see if it is a Flash-based design or an HTML-based design. Any Flash-based template will display the Flash logo on the bottom-left (**Figure 48b**).

Flash Logo

Figure 48b Use the Template Browser and Preview panels to examine the different Flash templates. Flash-based designs display a Flash logo at bottom of the Preview panel.

For cases where two templates use the same name, but one has the suffix "- HTML" applied, you can assume its "twin" uses Flash technology. For the rest of the templates, you must use the preview to be sure.

Scrolling Galleries

As noted, the default Flash template uses a filmstrip-style layout, with thumbnails that scroll down the left side of the page. However, there are other variations on this theme available, such as the "Lightroom UI" template, which uses dark shades of gray, a larger photo preview, and a strip of thumbnails that run across the bottom of the screen (**Figure 48c**).

Figure 48c The Lightroom UI template uses Flash to create a layout reminiscent of the Lightroom user interface.

As with the Airtight galleries, Flash galleries also have a range of formatting options, but there are more controls per panel. Also similar to the Airtight galleries, when you change any of these settings, Lightroom will recalculate the look of your layout on the fly, so the changes may take a few seconds to appear.

Site Info panel—This panel provides options to add a title for the web page, information about the Collection and photos being used, and contact information for the photographer (**Figure 48d**).

130

Figure 48d The Site Info panel contains options to add several useful pieces of information to your Flash gallery.

Color Palette panel—This panel provides several options for modifying the colors of a Flash template, including: three levels of text; menu and header colors; background and page border colors; and controller colors (such as buttons, scroll bar, and so on). These options are shown in **Figure 48e**.

Figure 48e The Color Palette panel allows you to customize the gallery colors.

Appearance panel—This panel defines both the size of the main preview or large image and the thumbnail images, as well as add an identity plate if needed. Here, the thumbnail size has been increased to Large (**Figure 48f**). There is also a Layout control that changes the thumbnail layout, which is discussed in the "Paginated Galleries" section.

Figure 48f The Appearance panel is often used to specify the size of the Flash gallery's image preview and thumbnails.

Image Info panel—This panel provides options to display two labels beneath each large preview. These labels can display one of the following values: Caption (applied in the Library module's Metadata panel), Custom Text, Date, Equipment, Exposure, File Name, Sequence, or Title.

Output Settings panel—This panel allows you to define the (JPEG) quality of the thumbnails and preview; include copyright metadata or all metadata for each file; apply text or graphical watermarks to the large image; and apply output sharpening.

Paginated Galleries

Another type of Flash template available in Lightroom 3 uses what are called paginated layouts. Instead of using a scrolling strip of thumbnails across the left or bottom edges of the page, the thumbnails are grouped in rows and columns, just like the Airtight SimpleViewer's layout. To view an example of a paginated layout, you can use one of two methods:

Slideshow-Only Layouts

Generally, I don't use the Slideshow Only option (found in the Layout pop-up menu) for Flash galleries, because it doesn't provide viewers a chance to look through the thumbnails and choose shots individually. Even the Airtight AutoViewer provides a glimpse at the previous and next images in the "show," while Slideshow layouts only display the main image and a few controls. This is a matter of personal preference; others will prefer the simplicity and clean design of slideshows.

- Take a scrolling layout like the Lightroom UI template that was described earlier, and from the Appearance panel, use the Layout pop-up menu and choose Paginated. This produces a grid of thumbnails next to the large image preview, while maintaining the rest of the "Lightroom UI" look (**Figure 48g**).

Figure 48g You can arrange the thumbnails in any Flash gallery to operate as a grid using the Layout pop-up menu in the Appearance panel; just choose the Paginated option.

- Using the Templates Browser panel, roll the cursor over the different layouts and choose one of the available templates: Blue Sky, Clean, Earthy, Stationary, or Taxi.

All the same formatting options as described in the Scrolling Galleries section apply to paginated galleries. The main difference to keep in mind is that the number of thumbnail pages (seen on the left side of the layout) is defined by the number of images in the collection and the Thumbnail Images setting in the Appearance panel.

#**49** Share Photos on Flickr

For the uninitiated, Flickr.com is a website owned by Yahoo! that provides a variety of methods for uploading, modifying, and sharing your digital photos. Signing up for an account is free, and while not the only site of its kind, Flickr is quite popular and easy to use. This tip will show you the new capabilities in Lightroom 3 that integrate directly with Flickr, so you can upload files directly from the Library module.

To get started with Flickr in Lightroom 3, open the Publish Services panel (from the Library module—left panel group) and click the Flickr Set Up button. This opens the Lightroom Publishing Manager that displays a series of settings for Flickr that need to be configured (**Figure 49a**).

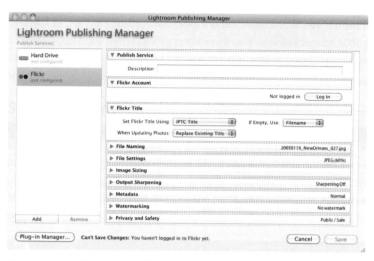

Figure 49a The Lightroom Publishing Manager provides all the settings you need to access your Flickr account and upload a selection of files from the Library module.

The following steps demonstrate how the Flickr process works in Lightroom. The only prerequisite is that you need to have signed up for an account on Flickr.com and have access to that account from the computer running Lightroom.

1. Give the Flickr Publish Service a name by filling in the Publish Service Description field (**Figure 49b**). This name will subsequently appear in the Publisher Services Manager List (left side) and on the Flickr button in the Publish Services panel; this will be illustrated later in the process.

(continued on next page)

Figure 49b Start by giving the Flickr publishing service module a name.

2. Log in to your Flickr Account by clicking the Log In button Not logged in (Log In) and then clicking the Authorize button when Lightroom displays the confirmation dialog box (**Figure 49c**).

Figure 49c Confirm Lightroom is authorized to log in to Flickr.

3. This will open your web browser, connect it to Flickr, and display a secondary authorization screen—this time confirming with Flickr that Lightroom has permission to access your account. Choose the second option (on the right) to confirm account access (**Figure 49d**).

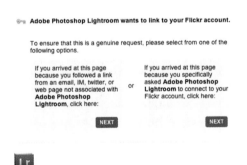

Figure 49d Authorize Flickr to interact with your copy of Lightroom.

4. A final confirmation screen will appear. Click OK, I'll Authorize It. Flickr will confirm the connection between Lightroom and Flickr (**Figure 49e**).

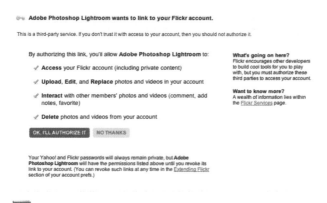

Figure 49e You can never have too many Flickr confirmation screens.

5. Switch back to Lightroom; you will revisit your Flickr page again later in the process. A new dialog box will be visible. Click the Done button. This will show a change of status in the Flickr Account settings, showing that you are now logged in to Flickr (**Figure 49f**).

Figure 49f Once back in Lightroom, clicking Done will enable you to move forward with the file settings and export process.

6. The Flickr Title controls let you set a title or name for each image on the Flickr page itself. The options are to use the actual filename of the photo, use the title found in IPTC metadata, use no title, and determine whether the title is replaced if a file is updated from Lightroom (**Figure 49g**).

Figure 49g Image titles that are displayed on Flickr.com can be defined in Lightroom.

(continued on next page)

7. Under File Naming, click the Rename To option to customize the names of the files you will be uploading. If you use date-and-subject style filenames for the originals on your hard drive (such as 05252009_NewYorkCity.dng), this option is helpful because it lets you create more web-friendly names for the web output. I find the Custom Name – Sequence option in the pop-up menu quite useful (**Figure 49h**).

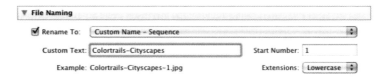

Figure 49h Giving your files more web-friendly names can be important.

8. Under File Settings, choose the JPEG format quality setting. Values between 60 and 80 usually produce the best compromise between small files and good quality (**Figure 49i**). If you have a strict size limit in mind, select the Limit File Size To check box and type in the amount (in Kilobytes).

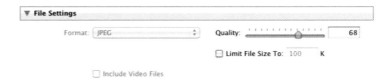

Figure 49i Set the JPEG format quality of the size and appearance of your photos.

9. Use the Image Sizing controls to define the dimensions of your photos. Typically, photographers will choose the Long Edge option and set a value such as 640 or 800 pixels (**Figure 49j**) because it is Flickr-friendly.

Figure 49j Resize your images so they fit within the confines of Flickr small layout.

10. If you wish to make your images crisper when displayed online, open the Output Sharpening controls, select the Sharpen For check box, then choose the Screen option and an Amount value (**Figure 49k**).

Figure 49k Sharpening options are available if needed.

11. If necessary, choose to include only basic image metadata and/or a watermark with your published Flickr images (**Figure 49l**).

Figure 49l Metadata for each image can be minimized and a watermark preset applied.

12. Choose your Flickr sharing and safety options (**Figure 49m**).

Figure 49m Set your sharing and safety options before uploading so that only those you want to view your photos can do so once uploaded.

13. Click Save. This will create your Flickr Photostream (a view where you can drag files from the Grid view or Filmstrip) in the Publish Services panel. Click your Photostream (**Figure 49n**). It will be empty by default.

Figure 49n Once your Flickr publish settings are saved, you can click your Photostream. (This is like Flickr's version of a collection.) By default it will be empty.

(continued on next page)

14. Finally, from the Grid view or Filmstrip, select and drag the files you want to share onto the Photostream icon. An orange highlight will appear (**Figure 49o**).

Figure 49o Drag the thumbnails of the photos you wish to share onto the Photostream.

You can then click the Photostream icon and all the files you added will appear in its own Grid view (**Figure 49p**).

Figure 49p Once you see all the images you want to upload in the Photostream view, click the Publish button. After a short wait, you should see all the shots on Flickr!

15. When you're ready to upload the photos, click Publish and you're finished. After a few moments your shots should appear on Flickr.com under the Photostream section.

CHAPTER FOUR

Perfecting Images in Photoshop CS5

For photographs that have been edited in Lightroom or ACR but need further fine-tuning before creating print or web output, Photoshop CS5 offers an impressive array of tools, adjustments, and transformations. It would be easy to fill this entire book with only Photoshop tips, but of course the idea is to provide a full picture of the digital workflow.

In that spirit, I've identified over 50 tips designed to help you work more efficiently with existing tools and functions, and to apply creative effects with new features like Puppet Warp and improved features like Merge to HDR Pro.

The beauty of digital editing is that experimenting with Photoshop usually feels more like fun than work. Books and videos are important guideposts, but ultimately the best way to master Photoshop is to really dig into the tools and see which tools best suit your photographic or creative goals. If you recently upgraded from Photoshop CS3 or CS4, you may wonder what you can do with CS5 that you can't also accomplish in ACR or Lightroom. The following list covers just a few examples:

- Seamlessly blending photos to create HDR and panoramic images

- Nondestructively warping and transforming subjects in an image

- Creating photo illustrations that mimic real paint media

- Selectively blurring a composition to refocus the viewer's attention

Chapter 4 starts with important tips for customizing your workspace and setting up Photoshop for better performance. You will also learn useful shortcuts for working with various tools and for quickly finding images using the new Mini Bridge panel. The rest of the chapter covers a wide range of tips designed to help you maximize the quality of your photography. A general familiarity with basic imaging concepts, such as layers, channels, and selections is assumed. Where necessary, tips that are specific to Photoshop CS4 or CS5 will be noted.

#50 Setting Preferences

Customizing Photoshop

This section includes Tips #50 through #54 and focuses on getting Photoshop CS5 set up quickly for a photography workflow. This is, of course, not an exhaustive listing, but the next five tips can go a long way toward making Photoshop a more efficient and intuitive imaging platform.

Once you have installed Photoshop CS5 and you're ready to explore the application or start working with your photos, you may want to take a few minutes to customize your preferences.

General Preferences

You can open Photoshop's Preferences dialog box by pressing Command-K (Mac OS) or Control-K (Windows). Alternatively, you can open the Preferences dialog box by choosing Photoshop > Preferences > General (Mac OS) or Edit > Preferences > General (Windows). Any of these techniques will display Photoshop's General preferences (**Figure 50a**).

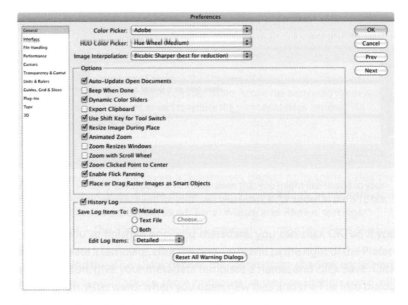

Figure 50a Photoshop's General Preferences is a good place to start.

The settings shown in Figure 50a are what I typically use. The key settings follow:

Color Picker (Adobe)—This is the default value and ensures all the features and tools, which provide a means of choosing a color, use the Adobe Color Picker (**Figure 50b**), rather than the Mac OS or Windows color pickers, which are somewhat less capable in my opinion.

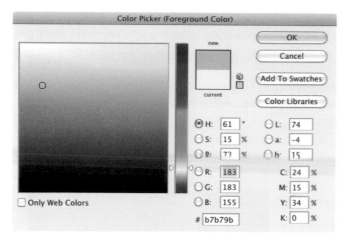

Figure 50b The Adobe Color Picker provides additional options and more precision when compared to the Mac OS and Windows color pickers.

HUD Color Picker (Hue Wheel [Medium])—This is a new capability in Photoshop CS5 that allows you to choose colors by calling up a temporary color picker that hovers over your document at the location of your cursor (**Figure 50c**). The HUD picker concept is covered in detail in Tip #57.

Figure 50c The HUD Color Picker is new in Photoshop CS5 and provides a more efficient means of selecting colors while working on your photos.

Image Interpolation (Bicubic Sharper)—This setting determines the default method of image scaling or resizing for features like the Crop tool and Image Size command. If you choose a suboptimal method here, it can result in degraded details or artifacts when you resize your images later. Because I reduce the size of my original photos far more often than I enlarge them, I choose Bicubic Sharper. If you frequently enlarge photos, choose Bicubic Smoother.

Use Shift Key for Tool Switch (On)—When selected, this option ensures that the Shift key must be held down in order to switch among tools that are grouped together in the Tools panel. For example, the Brush Tool, the Pencil Tool, the Color Replacement Tool, and the new Mixer Brush Tool are grouped together in the Tools panel (**Figure 50d**).

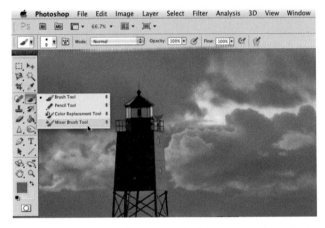

Figure 50d You can switch among tools that are grouped together in the Tools panel by pressing Shift and the tool's shortcut key (for example, Shift-B cycles through the tools that are grouped with the new Mixer Brush).

To invoke the most recently used tool in this group, you can press the B key at any time during your edits, but to switch to one of the other tools in this group, you must press Shift-B and repeat until the tool icon you need is displayed. If this preference is turned off, you can inadvertently switch tools by double-tapping the shortcut key.

Resize Image During Place (On)—This setting is used in conjunction with the Place command (File > Place), which takes one image and adds it to another image as a new Smart Object layer. When this setting is on, and the image being placed is larger than the target image or uses the opposite orientation, Photoshop will resize the long edge of the placed photo so that it fits inside the canvas of the target photo.

Zoom Resizes Windows (Off)—I typically deselect this preference because it can reduce the number of times I need to resize a window. For example, it's not uncommon to expand a window to leave empty space around the image canvas. This allows you to see and access the periphery of the photo when you need to precisely place a selection, crop marquee, or perform a similar task. Leaving this preference deselected ensures that the window size remains the same even if you zoom out. If zoom resizing is selected, every time you change the magnification of the image, the window will automatically shrink to fit the image, leaving no space around the edges.

Zoom Clicked Point to Center (On)—This option determines if repeatedly clicking a specific region of your photo with the Zoom tool will automatically place that region at the center of your window or viewing area, as Photoshop zooms into the image detail. Selecting this preference can be quite helpful when you need to quickly evaluate a specific detail in the scene, because it reduces the amount of panning (or scrolling) necessary to move the targeted details to the center of your view. More zoom and pan methods are discussed in Tip #56.

Place or Drag Raster Images as Smart Objects (On)—New to Photoshop CS5, if this option is selected and you place an image or drag one into your open Photoshop document, the new image layer that is created will be a Smart Object. This can be useful if you have to scale the layer more than once during your edits, as it will better maintain the quality of the image being placed or dragged into your open file. Smart Objects and transforms are discussed in Tip #70.

Interface Preferences

There are also user interface preferences that can be used to further customize your Photoshop experience when editing photos. To access these preferences, click the Interface heading in the Preferences dialog box (left side). The setup I typically use is shown in **Figure 50e**.

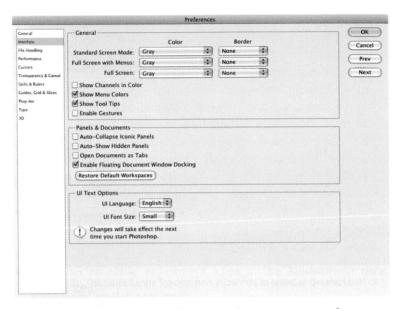

Figure 50e Photoshop's Interface preferences can be an important part of streamlining your workflow.

Screen Mode Colors and Borders (Set all Colors to Gray and all Borders to None or Line.)—This ensures consistency when viewing photos in expanded windows and full-screen modes, because the background will be a neutral gray, and there will be no distracting drop shadows around the edges of your image.

Show Tool Tips (On)—Selecting this option ensures that whenever you mouse over a tool icon or other clickable feature in Photoshop, a small tool tip will appear after a few seconds.

Auto-Collapse Iconic Panels (Off)—When this setting is selected, if you open a panel from its docked icon and then click somewhere else in the photo or UI, the iconic panels will close. For this reason, it may be helpful to leave this preference deselected so that as you make adjustments, you can see the changes in the panel. For laptop users with limited screen space, leaving this setting selected can save space.

Open Documents as Tabs (Off)—Unless you prefer that all the documents you open share a common window by default (much the way tabs share a single window in many web browsers), you may want to leave this setting off. This setting is specific to Photoshop CS4 and CS5.

Enable Floating Document Window Docking (On)—The combination of selecting this option and deselecting the Open Documents as Tabs option will give you the best of both worlds—the ability to dock windows together when you need to, but by default open all images in a separate window (**Figure 50f**). To learn more about working with tabbed documents, check Tip #58. This setting is specific to Photoshop CS4 and CS5.

Figure 50f Deselecting Open Documents as Tabs, in combination with allowing floating windows to be docked manually, provides more flexibility than always opening images as tabs inside an open window, or never using tabbed documents.

File Handling Preferences

To open the File Handling preferences, click the File Handling heading in the Preferences dialog box (**Figure 50g**).

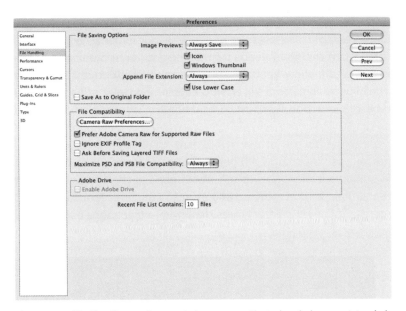

Figure 50g File Handling preferences help to ensure Photoshop behaves as intended when saving or opening certain file formats.

Image Previews (Always Save)—Choosing this setting from the pop-up menu ensures that a JPEG preview will always be saved with your files so that you can look at them in other applications like the Mac OS Finder.

Append File Extension (Always Save)—Choosing this setting from the pop-up menu ensures you will always be able to see your files' extensions at a glance and determine the file format.

Save As to Original Folder (Off)—This option is new in Photoshop CS5 and allows the last folder to which you saved to be set as the default location, rather than the same folder the images were opened from. For example, you may store all your raw files from a shoot in one folder. Turning this preference off before opening the next raw file from that folder means that when you're finished with the file and ready to save it in Photoshop, the application will default to the last folder you saved to, rather than the folder with all your raw files.

Prefer Adobe Camera Raw for Supported Raw Files (On)—When selected, this setting ensures that ACR will always open your supported raw file types and DNG files when you double-click them, rather than them opening in a third-party application.

Ask Before Saving Layered TIFF Files (Off)—Since TIFF and PSD are the two most popular formats for image editing, and since using layers is often required, deselecting this option can save you the annoyance of dismissing a dialog box every time you save a layered TIFF file. You might want to leave this option selected for publishing workflows where some applications don't support layered TIFF data.

Maximize PSD and PSB File Compatibility (On)—When selected, this option ensures that Lightroom is able to recognize and display files that have been edited and saved in Photoshop CS5.

Performance Preferences

To open Photoshop CS5's Performance preferences, click the Performance heading in the Preferences dialog box. These preferences are especially important for maximizing Photoshop performance based on your computer hardware. Aside from being a fully 64-bit application, the way Photoshop handles Cache Settings has evolved somewhat, so it's worth taking a look at some typical settings, in this case for a computer that has 8GB of RAM installed and a dedicated Scratch Disk (**Figure 50h**).

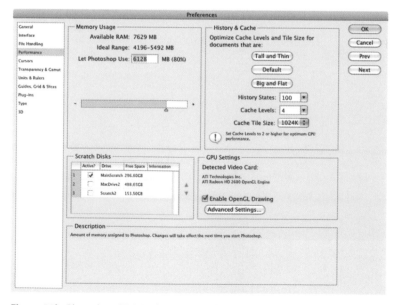

Figure 50h Photoshop CS5's Performance preferences.

About 64-Bit

The main thing to remember about Photoshop's 64-bit capabilities is that it means you can now allocate much larger amounts of RAM to the application than you could previously. Essentially, the only limitations are how much RAM your computer can use, and how many other applications will need to share that RAM simultaneously with Photoshop.

Performance Preference Help

If you roll the mouse over any of the controls in the Performance preferences area, you will get a description of what that function does in the Description area.

Memory Usage—This setting is system dependent. The RAM value to choose will depend on how much memory you have installed. The more you can allocate (while leaving at least 1-2GB for other applications that may use RAM simultaneously) the better. Here, slightly more than 6GB of RAM have been assigned. This is important because it means most files and operations can be carried out completely in RAM, speeding things up.

Scratch Disks—This value is system dependent. If possible, choose an internal disk that is formatted and completely empty. Alternatively, you can choose a (hopefully fast) external drive that is empty, if one is available. You can think of this as Photoshop's "scratchpad" where it can temporarily write and store information as it is calculating solutions to the edits you are performing. Having a dedicated scratch disk can greatly improve Photoshop performance.

History & Cache—These values are workflow dependent. If you often create documents that have smaller dimensions but many layers, click the Tall and Thin button. If you create files with large dimensions but only a few layers, click the Big and Flat button. For all other uses, clicking the Default button should provide good results.

#51 Defining Color Settings

A vital part of setting up Photoshop is making sure that your RGB Working Space (discussed shortly) is matched to the working space you used in the Lightroom Export settings (Tip #37) and the ACR Workflow Options (Tip #40). To define how Photoshop handles the colors in your photos, choose Edit > Color Settings, or press Shift-Command-K (Mac OS) or Shift-Control-K (Windows) to open the Color Settings dialog box (**Figure 51**). To show all the options, click the More Options button.

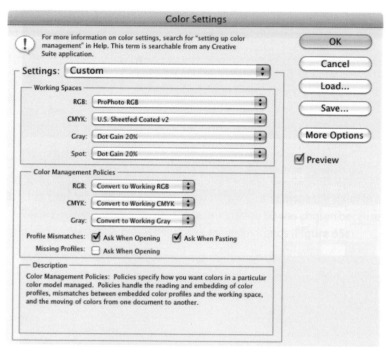

Figure 51 Photoshop CS5's Color Settings dialog box allows you to set the Working Spaces (or Color Spaces) for each type of workflow that you might use.

Settings—This pop-up menu allows you to select either a preset that contains specific settings for all the working (color) spaces or select any custom presets that you have saved. Figure 51 shows a custom preset that uses the same RGB working space as Lightroom. To create a preset, choose your settings, click the Save button, name your preset, give it a description if needed, and click OK.

ICC Color Profiles

Applications like Photoshop, ACR, and Lightroom use system-level files called ICC Color Profiles to define the color-working range of hues, tones, and color shades that will be available to you when editing a particular file.

ProPhoto RGB, Adobe RGB (1998), and *sRGB IEC61966-2.1* are all examples of color spaces that you can use with Photoshop to suit a particular workflow, and which are defined by ICC Color Profiles that use the same names.

ICC stands for International Color Consortium. You can learn more about the ICC and color management at http://www.color.org/.

Working Spaces (RGB Working Space)—Referencing the setup described in Tips #37 and/or Tip #40, in most cases you'll want to choose either ProPhoto RGB or Adobe RGB (1998) for this setting. Use the latter for workflows where you might be sharing your files with third parties.

Color Management Policies—Although color management is a topic that could fill its own book, the main concerns here are making sure that Photoshop follows the desired behaviors when it encounters a file that has no color profile or has a profile that does not match your active working space. The safest (but most time-consuming) route is to preserve any embedded profiles for documents you receive, and then decide—at the time you open the document—how to handle that profile mismatch. You may want to discuss the best option for you with any service providers that you work wIth, such as prInt bureaus.

#52 Simplifying the Menus

One of the most useful customizations you can make to Photoshop's user interface is simplifying the keyboard shortcuts. Photoshop's menus are packed with dozens of commands, adjustments, and functions for image editing, but it's rare that any one user needs to use them all on a regular basis. To "revive" them anytime, you might need to look over the full menu.

Customizing the Main Menu

To customize the main menu in Photoshop, choose Edit > Menus. This opens the Keyboard Shortcuts and Menus dialog box (**Figure 52a**). Here, the menu customization options for Photoshop CS5 Extended are shown; in Photoshop CS5 Standard, there is no Analysis or 3D menu.

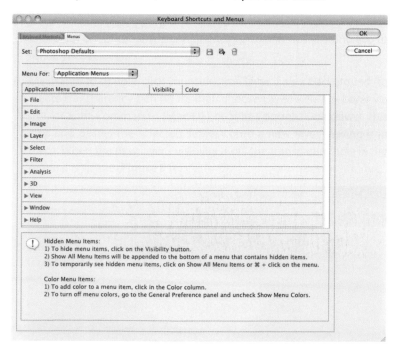

Figure 52a   The Photoshop Keyboard Shortcuts and Menus dialog box provides options for streamlining your workflow.

To customize your menus, click the disclosure triangle next to the word "File" (this represents the File menu), or whichever menu you want to start with. Once identified, click the eyeball icon next to each item you do not want to show in the menu (**Figure 52b**).

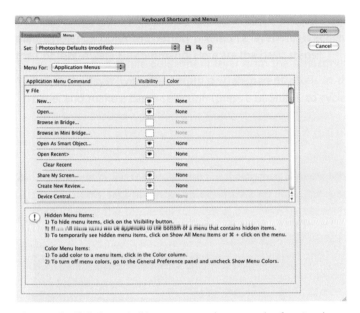

Figure 52b Click the eyeball icon next to each command or function that you wish to hide in the menu being customized.

Here, the commands for Browse in Bridge, Browse in Mini Bridge, and Device Central have been hidden. The resulting menu is shown next to the default File menu in **Figure 52c**.

Figure 52c Removing just a few commands or functions can make a menu easier to use.

Figure 52d shows two additional menus that were simplified. For example, the Check Spelling and Find and Replace Text commands have been hidden within the Edit menu, as well as the Define Pattern command. In the Image menu, Calculations, Variables, Apply Data Set, and Trap have all been hidden.

Figure 52d Additional menu customizations can speed your workflow further. When finished, all the changes can be saved as a preset.

When you're finished customizing all the menus, click the Save button, Set: Photoshop Defaults (modified) , give your custom menu preset a name, and click OK. As you make additional changes, you can resave using the same name by just clicking the Save button again.

Customizing Panel Menus

If you want to customize a specific panel pop-up menu (for example, the Layers panel pop-up), you can do that by opening the Menu For pop-up menu, Menu For: Panel Menus , and choosing Panel Menus. From there you can scroll through the list, find your panel, and follow the same steps for removing items and saving those changes as part of your preset (**Figure 52e**).

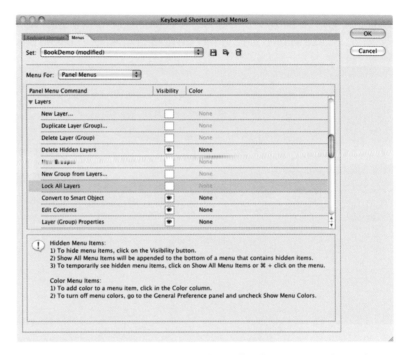

Figure 52e Panel menus can be customized as well as the main menu. This can be very useful for complex menus like the Layers panel pop-up.

#**53** Custom Keyboard Shortcuts

Once Photoshop's menus have been customized to suit your workflow, the Keyboard Shortcuts and Menus dialog box (**Figure 53a**) can be used to customize your keyboard shortcuts. Click the Keyboard Shortcuts tab to get started, Keyboard Shortcuts | Menus. If the Keyboard Shortcuts and Menus dialog box isn't open, access it by choosing Edit > Keyboard Shortcuts.

Figure 53a Keyboard shortcuts in Photoshop are customized from the same dialog box as menu items.

Customizing Shortcuts for the Main Menu
Decide which shortcut you want to modify first, and then open the menu list that contains that shortcut. For example, if you'd like to customize the Step Backward and Step Forward commands, open the Edit list. From there you can assign a shortcut by clicking the default keystroke that is listed (**Figure 53b**).

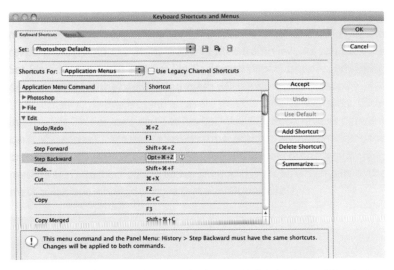

Figure 53b Once the appropriate menu list is opened, click the shortcut's keystroke to select that command or function.

Next, press the keystroke that you want to use. The new keystroke appears in the shortcut field; if that combination of keys is already in use, a conflict warning is displayed (**Figure 53c**). To overwrite that shortcut, click the Accept button. This will apply the changes to the shortcut and display its new value; repeat as necessary.

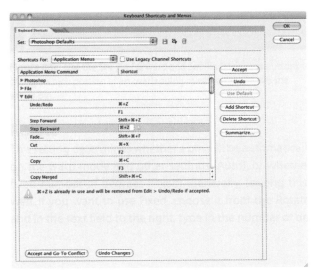

Figure 53c
Click Accept to dismiss any warning that may appear.

You can also click Accept and Go to Conflict, (Accept and Go To Conflict) , to accept your new shortcut and jump to the menu item that previously used the shortcut to set a new keystroke. You can undo a keystroke that you enter by clicking Undo. Once you have customized your shortcuts, you can save them as a set that will appear in the pop-up menu. Click the Save button, name the set, and then click Save.

Customizing Tools Panel Shortcuts

By default, most of the tools in Photoshop's Tools panel have single letter shortcuts. If you need to repurpose a shortcut by assigning it to a new tool, open the Shortcuts pop-up menu and choose Tools (**Figure 53d**).

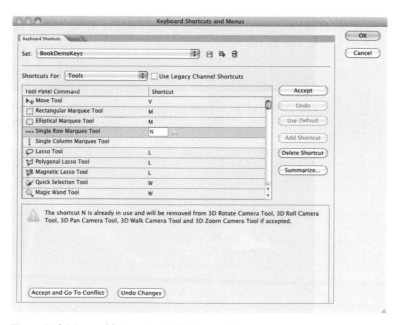

Figure 53d It is possible to customize Tools panel shortcuts.

Customize the shortcuts using the same steps noted earlier, but be aware that you cannot use the same shortcut for tools that are not grouped together. For example, by default the Count tool uses the shortcut I. If you assigned the shortcut C to the Count tool, the shortcut C would not be available to its default group (Crop, Slice, and Slice Select).

#54 Using Mini Bridge

You're probably aware that Bridge is an advanced file browser (with access to ACR for raw files) that is designed to apply various attributes to files so that they can be categorized, sorted, and searched. The primary differences between Lightroom and Bridge are the Bridge user interface and Bridge's ability to handle many file types.

One caveat is that it can be inefficient to frequently switch back and forth between Photoshop and Bridge to find the files you need. This drawback has been resolved in Photoshop CS5 with the new Mini Bridge panel. Mini Bridge is an extension of Bridge CS5 that uses a panel to provide quick access to its basic file-browsing and sorting capabilities. By default, when you open Photoshop, you should be greeted by the Essentials workspace; Mini Bridge is a part of this workspace. To open Mini Bridge (**Figure 54a**), click the icon panel that displays a folder with the letters "Mb" on it,

Figure 54a When you first open Mini Bridge, you will have the option to start browsing files from Bridge CS5 immediately or set the Mini Bridge preferences (Settings).

If you click the Browse Files button, Bridge CS5 launches in the background, and a few seconds later, the Mini Bridge UI comes to life with options for looking through your photographs. You may need to drag the edges of the panel outward, so that you can see its controls and options more clearly (**Figure 54b**).

Figure 54b Mini Bridge provides its own panels (or *pods*) for navigating folders, scrolling through thumbnails, and previewing individual files.

Navigation Pod

The primary means for choosing folders and series of images in Mini Bridge is the Navigation Pod, located near the top-left portion of the panel. This pod works as a split viewer and displays four types of image sources: Favorites, Recent Folders, Recent Files, and Collections. When you click an option, Mini Bridge displays the contents on the right side of the view (**Figure 54c**).

Bridge Favorites

To set Bridge CS5's Favorites, open the application, press Command-K (Mac OS) or Control-K (Windows), and under General preferences, choose from the available Favorites options.

Figure 54c Mini Bridge's Navigation Pod displays content from Bridge CS5's Favorites panel, Collections panel, and recently used folders and files lists.

Another means of navigating with Mini Bridge is to use the built-in Path Navigator widget, located just above the Navigation Pod. This feature allows you to see the path of your currently visible folder, including intermediate folders that you can search by clicking the small chevrons to the right of each folder icon (**Figure 54d**). You can also click once on any folder icon in the path to jump to that folder in the path hierarchy.

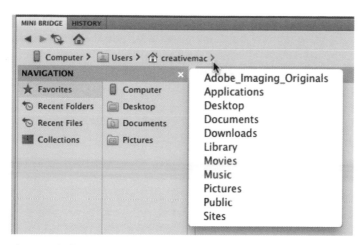

Figure 54d The Path Navigator in Mini Bridge provides another easy way of searching through your folder hierarchy.

Content Pod

To view, scale, sort, or filter through your thumbnails, the Content Pod provides most of the tools you will need to find your images quickly. **Figure 54e** details the function for each icon.

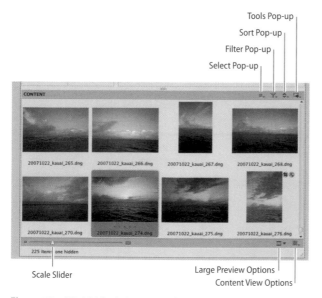

Figure 54e Mini Bridge's Content Pod.

Preview Pod

To preview an image at a larger size inside the panel, click the file and it will appear in the Preview Pod (**Figure 54f**). If you do not see the Navigation or Preview pods by default, click the Pod pop-up menu and select them, .

Figure 54f The Preview Pod is a great way to get a clearer idea of whether a specific photo meets your criteria. To resize the preview inside the pod, drag the resize handles. To get a full-screen preview, press the Space bar.

Tools

The Tools pop-up menu provides access to frequently used Photoshop workflows. For example, a great way to get started with an HDR workflow is to select your bracketed exposures in Mini Bridge, and then choose Merge to HDR Pro from the Tools pop-up menu (**Figure 54g**).

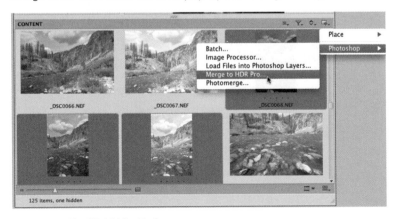

Figure 54g The Mini Bridge Tools pop-up menu.

#55 Using Live Preview Rotation

When editing pictures in Photoshop, there are two tools that can make the process of "maneuvering around" your photo more efficient. One is the Rotate View tool, , introduced in Photoshop CS4. My favorite use for Rotate View arises when I need to paint or mask along a contour that extends from the right half of the image toward the upper-left corner.

This can be difficult to mimic with a long brushstroke because I am right-handed (our wrists didn't evolve to handle this type of motion efficiently—we either have to pick up our hand and move the stylus, or extend the stylus' reach with our fingers, both can be awkward). Go ahead and try it! Notice which types of contours are easiest to mimic with your dominant hand as you make long brushstrokes. **Figure 55a** shows an image with problematic lines and contours.

Useful Workflow Shortcuts

The next six tips provide different means of quickly accessing powerful features that can speed up the process of painting, evaluating image detail, choosing colors precisely, grouping photos to save space, and accessing important document information.

Figure 55a Sometimes painting or masking around an object in your scene can be difficult because of the subject's orientation relative to how your hand moves the stylus.

To resolve this problem, you can spin the image preview between brushstrokes (without rotating the canvas), so that the difficult contours become properly oriented to the natural movement of your hands when using a stylus. Press and hold the R key to temporarily invoke the Rotate View tool, then drag your document to rotate. Here, I rotated the masts and arms on the boat.

When you release the R Key, your brush tool remains active, so you can continue masking or painting (**Figure 55b**). Continue this process iteratively until your edits are complete. When you've finished masking or painting, press the Escape key to return the image preview to its normal orientation.

Figure 55b Once the image preview has been temporarily rotated, it becomes much easier to follow any complex contours with a brushstroke.

#56 Pan & Zoom Techniques

When working in Photoshop, it's important to be able to quickly find and examine details at high magnifications, especially with today's high-resolution DSLR files. This can be accomplished with a couple different techniques that use the Hand tool and the Zoom tool with the new Scrubby Zoom option.

Hand Panning

Panning refers to the ability to scroll across parts of a document without having to use the document's scroll widgets. First, zoom to a magnification between 50 and 200% depending on the level of detail you need to see. Once you're zoomed in, press and hold the Space bar (this temporarily invokes the Hand tool), then drag the document to move it from side to side. If you have the Flick Pan preference selected (see Figure 50a), you can quickly "flick" your stylus to make the document scroll rapidly, like a sheet of paper being slid across a tabletop.

Scrubby Zoom

Photoshop CS5 has a new way to zoom in directly to the details you want to see. If you press Z to invoke the Zoom tool, you'll notice in the Options bar a Scrubby Zoom setting (**Figure 56**). If you select this option, you can place the Zoom tool directly over a specific image detail you want to view at high magnification, then drag to the right. This works like a zoom and pan feature with a single step.

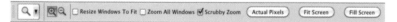

Figure 56 The new Scrubby Zoom allows you to focus on specific parts of your image more quickly by combining zoom and pan movements. This enables you to jump from one spot to the other without hand panning the document and then zooming.

Pan and Zoom Online

If you visit the home page for this book on Peachpit.com, you will find a video that provides a "live look" at how Hand Panning and Scrubby Zoom work.

#57 Using the HUD Color Pickers

Photoshop CS5 has two new HUD (or Heads Up Display) color pickers that enable you to choose colors on the fly, rather than having to visually target and click on the small color wells in the Tools panel.

Hue Strip

The Hue Strip looks and works much like the standard Color Picker dialog box, but without the various text fields. There is a strip along the right side for choosing the hue, and a square color ramp at left that allows you to choose a specific shade or tint for that hue.

1. To invoke the new color picker (Photoshop uses the Hue Strip setting by default), select one of the brush-based tools like the Clone Stamp, Dodge tool, or Mixer Brush and move the cursor over your document.

2. For Mac OS, press and hold Command-Alt-Control and click the document canvas; for Windows, press Shift-Alt-right-click on the canvas, and the new color picker appears over your cursor (**Figure 57a**).

Color Ramp

Hue Strip

Figure 57a The new Hue Strip color picker in Photoshop CS5 provides the ability to accurately select specific shades or tints of a given hue, directly over the cursor.

3. Release the keyboard shortcuts but keep the mouse down; the HUD will stay in place so that you can move your cursor around the color ramp to choose a specific shade or tint of the active hue (**Figure 57b**).

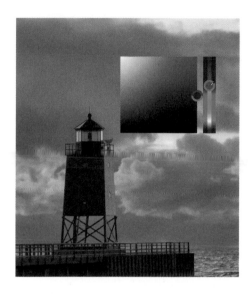

Figure 57b The Hue Strip allows you to change the hue range before picking a particular tint or shade of color based on that hue.

4. To change the hue value, mouse over to the hue strip, move the slider (for example, to change from red hues to orange hues), then move back to the ramp to choose the related color tint or shade (**Figure 57c**).

Figure 57c After setting your hue range, move the picker back to the ramp side of the HUD and choose the variation before releasing the mouse and continuing with your edits.

5. Release the mouse button (or pick up the stylus) to begin working.

Hue Wheel

The new HUD feature also provides access to a Hue Wheel color-picking method. Although it uses the same shortcuts and process as the Hue Strip, the Hue Wheel can make it easier to choose a precise hue because it expands the color spectrum over a larger area. Essentially, it provides a more subtle gradient as it moves from one hue to the next.

To use the Hue Wheel instead of a strip, open Photoshop's preferences by pressing Command-K (Mac OS) or Control-K (Windows). Under the HUD Color Picker, choose from the three sizes of Hue Wheel. Medium usually works well for most purposes unless you have a very small screen. The Hue Wheel (Medium) is shown in **Figure 57d**. It works the same way the strip does; the only difference is that the hues are distributed differently.

Figure 57d The Hue Wheel can be a more accurate way of selecting hues, though it also will cover more of your document.

#58 "Docking" Multiple Photos

As mentioned in Tip #50 and Figure 50e, you can set up Photoshop to open files in their own window by default, but also allow you to group files into a single window afterward if you need to save space. This capability is specific to Photoshop CS4 and CS5.

1. Under Interface preferences, deselect Open Documents as Tabs and select Enable Floating Document Window Docking (Figure 50e).

2. Open three or more files. You should see three separate windows.

3. Drag a file by the title bar over another file; a blue highlight will appear (**Figure 58**). Release the document to create a pair of docked (or tabbed) images.

Figure 58 Docking images in the Standard Screen Mode can save space.

#59 Displaying File Information

Ruler Access

You can access the Ruler units by clicking Command-R (Mac OS) or Control-R (Windows) and right-clicking the ruler to change units (for example from inches to cm).

If you're working in Standard Screen Mode (where each file has its own window), there is a simple trick to display important information about the document on the fly. To do this, move your cursor to the bottom of the document, and click and hold the small triangle near the left side of the window.

This will open a small menu of options, the information for which you can view just to the left of the menu itself (**Figure 59**). A few of the more relevant options for photography workflows include:

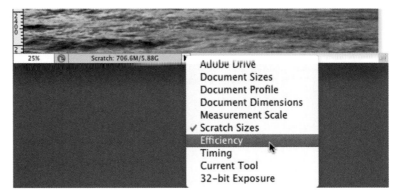

Figure 59 Having specific bits of information about the document displayed in the Status bar can be very helpful, especially when gauging resource usage or performance.

- **Document Profile**—This option displays the ICC color profile the document is tagged with, as well as the bits per channel.

- **Document Dimensions**—This option displays the width and height (or resolution) of the document, as well as the pixels per inch (or ppi), using the current ruler units.

- **Scratch Sizes** (shown)—This setting displays the amount of RAM being used for all currently open images (left), as compared to the total amount of RAM available for all images (right).

- **Efficiency**—This setting displays the percentage of time spent performing an operation instead of reading or writing to the scratch disk. If the value is below 100%, Photoshop is using the scratch disk and is therefore operating more slowly. Ideally, if you have enough RAM allocated, you may be able to avoid this for many workflows.

#60 Modifying IPTC Metadata

To access IPTC information from Photoshop, choose File > File Info to open the File Info dialog box. By default, it should open to the Description panel, which provides access to basic information fields like Document Title, Author, and Copyright Notice (**Figure 60a**). To add or change information, simply click in the individual fields and type the value. Note that this specific dialog box design was introduced in Photoshop CS4.

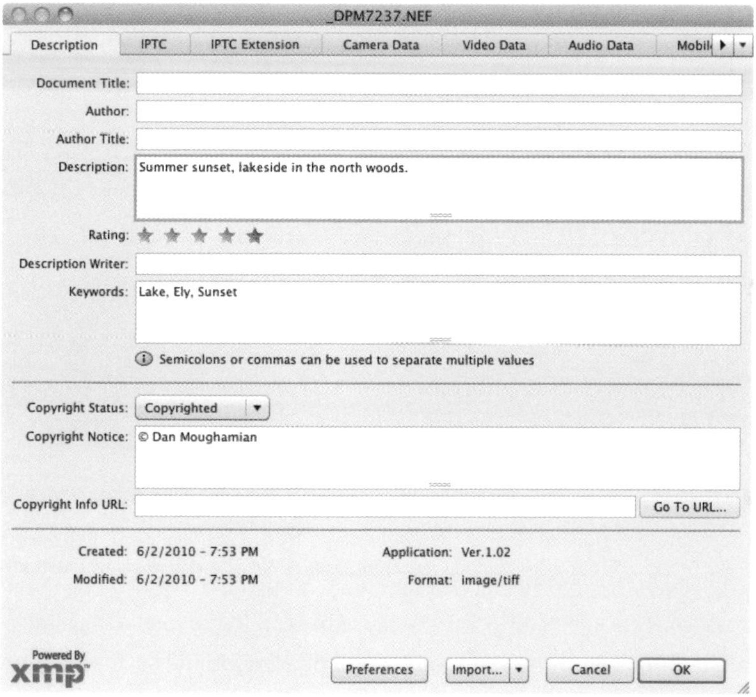

Figure 60a   The File Info dialog box.

Clicking the IPTC or IPTC Extension tabs will provide a much richer set of metadata values that you can supply for your photograph, if applicable, including several that could not fit in **Figure 60b**. Some of the information from the Description tab will carry over, as the two tabs share some common fields.

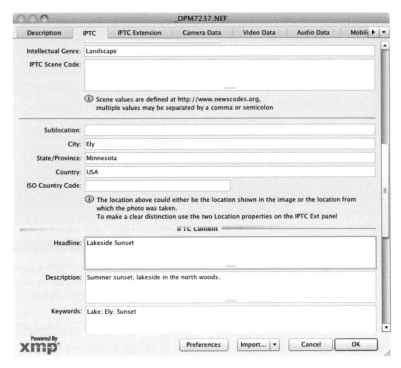

Figure 60b Virtually any type of IPTC information that you might like to add to your file for third-party reference and for your own reference can be added in the IPTC tab.

Once you've finished applying metadata, you can click OK, or, if you wish to create a template, click the pop-up menu to the right of the Preferences button, give your metadata template a name, and click Save. Click OK to finish. Afterward, when you open new files and the File Info dialog box, your template will be displayed in the same pop-up menu.

#61 Straightening Horizons with the Ruler Tool

Photoshop CS5 has a neat trick that allows you to define a horizon line and quickly crop the image in three quick steps.

1. Press Shift-I until the Ruler tool is selected, 📏 .

2. Click one side of the horizon, or an object in the scene you know to be level, and draw a line across to the other side (**Figure 61a**).

Selections, Masks, and Transformations

This section provides several tips for working with different kinds of transform edits, selection and masking workflows, and Smart Objects. The idea is not as much to cover the basics of how these processes work, as it is to demonstrate how to work with them more effectively.

Figure 61a You can use the Ruler tool in Photoshop CS5 to straighten photos.

3. Click the Straighten button in the Options bar. Photoshop will automatically rotate and crop the image (**Figure 61b**).

Figure 61b Once the horizon is defined, click the Straighten button to rotate and crop the image in a single step.

174

#62 Using Color Range Masks

The Color Range command is one of the best ways to make complex selections. Using color as the basis of a selection can often be quicker than trying to outline the subject with the Lasso tool or Pen tool. For this example, a black-and-white adjustment layer has been applied to the image, but the goal is to limit its effect to the areas behind the tree (**Figure 62a**).

Figure 62a The Color Range command is a good choice for creating layer masks.

1. Select the mask in the Layers panel, open the Masks panel, and click the Color Range button in to reveal the Color Range dialog box.

2. Often, the most effective way of gauging progress is to use the Image option for the dialog box preview and set the Selection Preview to either Black Matte or White Matte (**Figure 62b**).

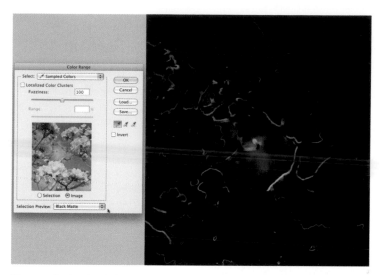

Figure 62b Set the dialog box's preview to Image and the Selection Preview (which is displayed on the document) to one of the matte options.

3. Turn Localized Color Clusters on and make sure the default Eyedropper is selected, . Then press and hold the Shift key and drag your cursor across the portions of the image you wish to select. Make several passes to ensure the initial selection is as accurate as possible.

For **Figure 62c**, the tree limbs and flowers are nearly pure black on the document preview, indicating they have been masked.

(continued on next page)

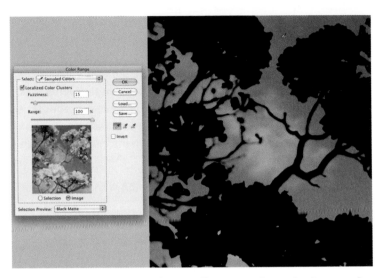

Figure 62c The Color Range Eyedroppers allow you to select or deselect part of the image for inclusion in the mask.

4. Click OK to see the final layer mask and the final effect (**Figure 62d**).

Figure 62d The final masked image adjustment.

#63 Converting Paths to Selections

You can use Bezier paths to create highly detailed and accurate selections. Once you've created and closed your path, and the Pen tool is still active, right-click the path and choose Make Selection to convert the path to a selection.

This opens the Make Selection dialog box (**Figure 63a**), where you can choose to add a feather value (in pixels) as well as create an anti-aliased selection (recommended in most cases when you are retouching). The final selection is shown in **Figure 63b**.

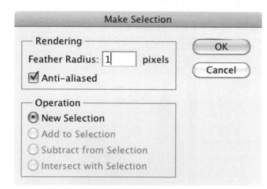

Figure 63a The Make Selection command allows you to set the parameters for your path-based selection to ensure it has smooth contours.

Figure 63b The final selection that was built from the path.

#64 Hybrid Lasso Selections

There are three Lasso tools and Lasso selection types that you can make, depending on whether you are selecting an object with organic-shaped edges, geometric edges, or high-contrast edges. Traditionally, the Lasso tool is used to make free-form organic selections, while the Polygonal Lasso is used to select hard-edged objects like stop signs or buildings. However, sometimes you will find subjects that have both straight edges and organic curves.

Luckily, there's a shortcut that allows you to use either the standard Lasso or Polygonal Lasso tool during the whole selection process, rather than switching back and forth. For this example, the outline of the architectural structure in **Figure 64a** provides both straight edges and rounded edges, so the Polygonal Lasso was the most logical starting point.

Figure 64a Some images provide the challenge of selecting areas that contain both straight-edged (or geometric) contours and rounded (or organic) contours. The Lasso tool and Polygonal Lasso tool can handle both types with a single shortcut.

1. Select the Polygonal Lasso tool by pressing the L key, or Shift-L to cycle through the Lasso group, if necessary.

2. Begin your selection by clicking a corner within your selection area and moving along a straight edge until you reach the next corner. Click a second time to anchor the polygon marquee to the second corner. Continue along the geometric contours until you reach a point where there is a curved edge.

3. As you reach an area with rounded or organic edges, press and hold the Alt key and draw around the edge freehand style, just as you would with the standard Lasso tool. Repeat this process as many times as necessary to complete the selection. The final result is shown in **Figure 64b**.

Figure 64b The final hybrid lasso selection area.

#65 Refining Selection and Mask Edges with Smart Radius

Adjust Edge settings

I generally avoid using the Adjust Edge controls when I'm working with Smart Radius, as they tend to work against the precision of a Smart Radius workflow. Therefore, you may find it useful with some images to use either Edge Detection settings with the Radius Refinement tools or the Adjust Edge controls, but not both.

One of the more powerful features in Photoshop is the Refine Edge command. It provides the ability to take a selection or layer mask and refine it so that the edge contours more precisely match the boundary of your subject. For Photoshop CS5, the Smart Radius feature has been added to further enhance edge refinement.

1. After you've made the initial selection (Color Range was used here), choose Select > Refine Edge. If you've made a layer mask, highlight the mask. Open the Masks panel and click the Mask Edge button. Either step will open the same dialog box for refining your edge work (**Figure 65a**). Alternatively, you can use Command-Alt-R (Mac OS) or Control-Alt-R (Windows).

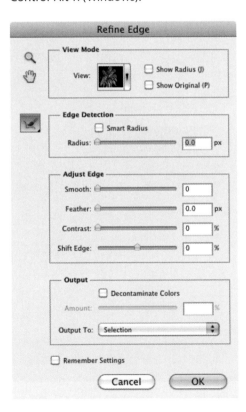

Figure 65a The Refine Edge dialog box provides powerful tools for tweaking and refining the smallest details of your selection edge (or mask edge).

2. Set the View pop-up menu to On Black (B) or On White (W) so the selection boundary can be seen clearly (**Figure 65b**). If there are black or white pixels in the selection or background, try Overlay (V).

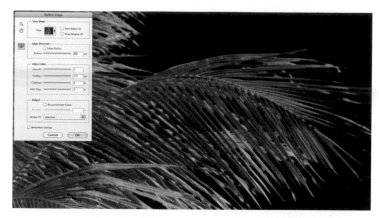

Figure 65b Changing the view type of your selection can make it easier to discern whether or not a specific setting or change has improved the selection.

3. Click the Smart Radius check box, ⬚ , and move the slider to a value between 30 and 50. Here, a value closer to 80 was chosen because it was necessary to reveal the tips of the palm fronds (**Figure 65c**).

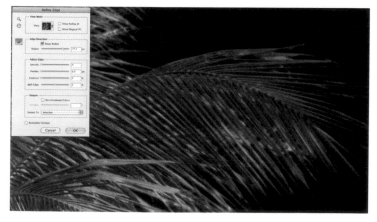

Figure 65c The initial use of Smart Radius for detecting selection edges can yield an immediate improvement in selection-edge (or mask-edge) quality.

(continued on next page)

4. By default, the Refine Radius tool is selected in the Refine Edge dialog box; if you mouse over the selection area, you should see a brush cursor with a small Plus (+) sign at the center. Use this brush to make a large brushstroke over the entire area you're trying to refine, including any extra background areas (**Figure 65d**).

Figure 65d Use the Refine Radius tool to brush over the areas that were improved by the Smart Radius value, but which are still showing minor flaws like details being truncated or background showing through.

5. The original selection should now have a more accurate edge. However, if you find that the contour is right but a few pixels are being excluded along the outer edges of your subject, you can nudge the Shift Edge slider (found in the Adjust Edge controls) to the right to include those excluded pixels along the entire selection edge. Alternatively, if a selection is a bit too wide, you can nudge the Shift Edge slider to the left to remove the extra pixels along the entire selection edge.

#66 Removing Color Casts from Selection and Mask Edges

Another important part of refining a selection or mask edge is removing color casts (also called *color contamination* when working with green screens and other color-key backdrops). This task is also accomplished within the Refine Edge/Refine Mask dialog box. This capability is specific to Photoshop CS5.

After refining the edge of your selection or mask with the Refine Radius tools as described in Tip #65, select the Decontaminate Color check box, 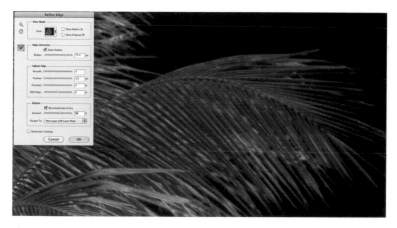, and experiment with slider values between 20 and 60. The objective is to maintain fine details in the selection while removing color casts (**Figure 66**). With a few tweaks, it should be possible to remove most if not all the unwanted color from the selection or mask edge.

Figure 66 After experimenting with the Smart Radius or Refine Radius, you should be able to include very fine details in your selection.

#67 Creating Smooth Textures: Clone and Patch

Using the Patch tool to replace textures with high-contrast boundaries can produce fuzzy results (**Figure 67a**). A quick way around this problem is to first use the Clone Stamp tool.

Figure 67a Patching areas with high-contrast edges can yield fuzzy results.

1. Select the Clone Stamp tool (press S or Shift-S to cycle through the tool group) and set a source from the surrounding area of texture. Clone over the high-contrast area. Don't worry if the look of the resulting texture or color doesn't "match" precisely. What matters most is minimizing the contrast between source and target areas, and creating some texture or pattern in the area to be corrected.

2. Select the Patch tool (J or Shift-J to cycle through the tool group). In the Options bar, make sure the Source radio button is selected.

3. Draw a selection with the Patch tool around the newly cloned, high-contrast area, then drag the selection to an area that has the desired appearance. For larger areas, use two or three patches. The end result should be a smooth, organic-looking correction (**Figure 67b**).

Figure 67b After cloning over the high-contrast area, using the Patch tool produces much smoother results in many cases.

#68 Enhancing Compositions with Content-Aware Scale

Introduced in Photoshop CS4, the Content-Aware Scale command provides a unique means of cropping without modifying or cutting away important details. **Figure 68a** shows the poolside scene.

Figure 68a A good candidate for Content-Aware Scale.

1. Duplicate the Background layer and rename the new layer Scale. Hide the Background before moving to the next step.

2. Using the Lasso tool (L), draw a selection around the areas that you would like Content-Aware Scale to protect while scaling the surrounding areas. Remember to press and hold the Shift key when you have finished one selection area and are moving to another.

3. Open the Channels panel and click the Save Selection as Channel button on the bottom of the panel (second from left). This will create a new alpha channel to protect the important details (**Figure 68b**).

Figure 68b Use the Channels panel to create a new alpha channel from your selection.

4. Open the Layers panel and click the Scale layer, then press Command-D (Mac OS) or Control-D (Windows) to deselect your protected areas.

5. Choose Edit > Content-Aware Scale. Note the Protect pop-up menu in the Options bar. Open it and choose the alpha channel you created. If you didn't explicitly give it a name, it will be called Alpha 1 unless you are working on a file with previously created alpha channels (**Figure 68c**).

Figure 68c Before scaling your image, be sure to select the newly created alpha channel from the Options bar by using the Protect pop-up menu.

6. Using the scale handles that are centered along the edges of the photo, nudge them inward until the image is the size and shape you want.

7. Make sure none of the other details in your image have become badly distorted and press Return or Enter. After the progress dialog box closes, you should see the finished result, with transparency in the cropped areas (**Figure 68d**).

Figure 68d The final scaled image, with both protected areas intact.

Handling Distortion

If the details in your scale region become distorted, you can try to remedy that by reducing the Amount value in the Options bar.

#69 Automated Lens Corrections

Adobe has also added a new kind of lens-correction process to Lightroom 3, ACR 6.1, and Photoshop CS5. These corrections are called *Profile Corrections* in Lightroom and ACR, and *Auto Corrections* in Photoshop CS5.

Essentially, a special chart is photographed using a rigorous procedure; this ultimately results in a camera-and-lens profile that describes, in digital terms, the kinds of distortions each lens design creates when used with a specific camera. This allows for rapid corrections that are generally quite accurate for more pronounced distortions, when an exact profile match is available. While these automated corrections are possible in Lightroom or ACR, thus far I prefer Photoshop's familiar UI.

1. To access Auto Correction, choose Filter > Lens Correction from the top portion of the menu. The Auto Correction tab should be selected by default (**Figure 69a**). If you wish, you can use Lens Correction as a Smart Filter by selecting your image layer in advance and choosing Filter > Convert to Smart Filter.

Figure 69a The Photoshop CS5 Lens Correction filter window displaying the new Auto Correction features.

2. To use the profiled correction, choose your brand of camera from the Camera Make pop-up menu, and choose a camera model and lens model from the Camera Model and Lens Model pop-ups, respectively.

Perfecting Images in Photoshop CS5

3. Once your profile is selected, choose which types of correction you would like applied to your image (**Figure 69b**). I generally recommend leaving Geometric Distortion, Chromatic Aberration, Vignette, and Auto Scale Image turned on.

Figure 69b After the profile is selected, choose the types of distortion you would like to fix and whether you would like Photoshop to automatically scale the image to remove any transparent areas.

That's all there is to it! If you have a matching profile or one that is a close approximation of your camera-lens combination, you should see the corrections immediately. Click OK to accept the changes.

#70 Smart Object Transforms

Since Photoshop CS4, the option to use image-transform commands nondestructively has been available by integrating them with Smart Object layers.

1. To maintain its integrity, duplicate the Background layer of your image and name it Transform; hide the Background when finished.

2. Right-click the Transform layer and choose Convert to Smart Object from the context menu.

3. Choose Edit > Transform > Distort. Here, Distort was chosen to help straighten the edges of the building (**Figure 70a**).

Figure 70a Once you've created a Smart Object layer, you can access any of the transform commands from the Edit menu to begin your nondestructive transforms.

4. Use the drag handles on the image to perform your desired transform edits (**Figure 70b**). Once finished, leave the drag handles active and go back to the Edit menu to invoke additional transform commands.

Figure 70b Each transform command provides handles for dragging portions of the document in a specific direction; multiple transforms can be used per session.

5. When finished, press Return (Mac OS) or Enter (Windows) to apply your transform edits. This may take a moment or two.

The best part is, if you decide you need to go back and modify your original transforms, you can do that by returning to the Edit menu and reinvoking the command(s) you originally used. The final corrected, cropped image is shown in **Figure 70c**.

Figure 70c Nondestructive image transforms and warps are now possible with Smart Object layers.

#71 Perspective Cropping

Many people don't realize that the Crop tool in Photoshop is also a type of transform tool, allowing you to correct minor horizontal and vertical distortions as part of the Photoshop workflow. To correct a vertical distortion (such as the illusion that a building or other structure appears to be "falling away" from the viewer), use these steps:

1. Select the Crop tool by pressing the C key or Shift-C.

2. Drag the crop marquee across the entire image.

3. Make sure the Crop Shield check box is selected and that its opacity is a relatively high number, ☑ Shield Color: ■ Opacity: 83% ▾ ☑ Perspective .

4. Using one of the corner points that is connected to the marquee edge, drag inward until the marquee edge and the subject edge are reasonably parallel (**Figure 71a**).

Figure 71a Use the edges of the crop marquee to maintain a more or less parallel relationship to the slanted edges.

5. Repeat Steps 4 and 5 with other distorted edges in the scene, then drag the edges back out to the edge of the scene (**Figure 71b**).

Figure 71b Once the perspective tweaks have been made, drag the crop marquee edges back to the edge of the frame.

6. Click Return (Mac OS) or Enter (Windows) to accept the perspective crop. The finished result is shown in **Figure 71c**.

Figure 71c The final results of a quick perspective crop can make a substantial difference in the quality of a photograph.

#72 HDR Pro: Exposure Tips

Multi-Exposure Workflows

This section includes five tips that focus on two of the more powerful (and frankly amazing) workflows in Photoshop CS5: Merge to HDR Pro and Photomerge. Each allows you to take multiple exposures and combine the files into a single shot. With Merge to HDR Pro, Adobe has created the makings of a class-leading solution for High Dynamic Range photography. It requires a good bit of hardware horsepower to run efficiently, but it's well worth any waiting involved. Photomerge is designed to help you create beautiful and seamless panoramas in a very short time, and it does that job extremely well.

Before you ever get to the stage of using Merge to HDR Pro, there are several photographic processes to consider when you're setting out to photograph a scene for HDR output:

- Use your DSLR's exposure-bracketing feature. The camera can incrementally change the shutter speed and snap several pictures much quicker than any photographer can. For more information on bracketing, consult your camera's owner manual.

  Typically, HDR photos are captured as a series of 3, 5, or 7 exposures. For most scenarios, 5 exposures should work well and keep your memory card from filling up too fast. For scenes with only moderate differences between the brightest highlights and midtones, 3 exposures should work. For darker scenes that have very bright details, 7 exposures may be needed.

- Do *not* change the aperture value from one shot to the next in a given series of bracketed exposures. If you do, the final quality of the merged HDR file will suffer due to inconsistent sharpness and potentially, artifacts. Photoshop may also have trouble aligning the photos precisely in some cases.

  Use the Aperture Priority mode and your depth-of-field preview to find the right level of sharpness for each scene and go with that setting for each set of bracketed exposures you take for that scene.

- If your DSLR supports it, use the *full-frame* or *matrix*-metering mode, where the camera considers all elements of the scene when determining the exposure values. Remember, you don't need to worry about exposing for a small area in the scene because chances are good in at least one of your bracketed shots, that area will be correctly exposed.

- Use a tripod or a lens that supports vibration reduction if at all possible. Even a slight blur from one photo to the next can cause problems when merging shots into a single HDR exposure.

- If you're shooting raw photos, see Tip #36 for things to keep in mind when preprocessing those files in Lightroom or ACR.

#73 HDR Pro: Creating the File

Once your bracketed exposures have been taken, imported to your computer, and preprocessed (color temperature, noise reduction, chromatic aberration, and so on), it's time to merge them together. Choose File > Automate > Merge to HDR Pro to invoke the Merge to HDR Pro dialog box. This feature has been significantly enhanced in Photoshop CS5.

Choose the appropriate options, based on how you have organized the bracketed exposures on your hard drive. Click the Browse button to open your system-file dialog box, so that you can find and select your bracketed shots. Once you open them, the file names will appear in the dialog box (**Figure 73**).

A Few Words about HDR

Most photographers are intimately familiar with limitations of modern cameras. Often we encounter scenes with a high dynamic range that forces us to "expose for the highlights" or "expose for the shadows," depending on what our goal is. But something is usually left behind by the camera when we do that; detail is lost in the other parts of the scene. High Dynamic Range (HDR) workflows attempt to solve this problem by using a series of exposures (each capturing a different part of the scene's tonal range) to create a single, highly detailed image that displays "correct exposure" for all areas of the scene.

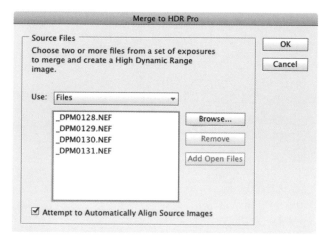

Figure 73 The Merge to HDR Pro dialog box facilitates the process of bringing your files together and aligning them when Photoshop merges them together.

As a final step, choose the Attempt to Automatically Align Source Images option. This can help handheld shots in particular, where the camera may have moved slightly from one exposure to the next.

#74 HDR Pro: Tone Mapping

After processing the original exposures, the Merge to HDR Pro user interface appears in a modal window (**Figure 74a**).

Figure 74a The Merge to HDR Pro window.

Tone Mapping Mode

By default, Merge to HDR Pro displays options and controls for a 16-bit, Local Adaptation workflow or *mode*. Because this combination offers the most powerful features for defining the look of an HDR image, and because it provides an easy segue to a 16-bit editing process, this is the mode I recommend.

There are also options for 8- and 32-bit output, and three additional conversion options for both 8- and 16-bit modes: Equalize Histogram (an automatic "averaging" of the data); Exposure & Gamma (uses a Gamma slider to set the white point and an Exposure slider to handle brightness); and Highlight Compression (automatic "averaging" that attempts to avoid clipped highlights, usually resulting flat-looking images).

Remove Ghosts

The next step is to decide if the Remove Ghosts option is required (located just above the Mode pop-up menu), ☐ Remove ghosts ┌─ Mode: 16 Bit . For HDR, *ghosts* refer to a faint blurring effect that can occur when Photoshop tries to reconcile areas of the frame that contain subject matter that changes position slightly from one exposure to the next. Leaves blowing in the wind, water flowing past the camera, and passing clouds are all scenarios that might produce ghost artifacts. **Figure 74b** shows subtle wave details added back to the surface of the lake that were previously blurred.

> **Ghosts: Base Image**
>
> You can choose which exposure will serve as the basis for your ghost correction. Just click on a thumbnail to choose it as the base image.

Figure 74b Use the Remove Ghosts option to make sure that areas in the frame with moving subjects are not blurred.

Tone & Detail

Tone & Detail controls are analogous to the Basic panel controls in Lightroom or ACR (Tip #25) and serve a similar purpose.

Gamma—This slider helps establish the overall tonal balance of the
scene and is often useful—when used in combination with the Exposure
and Highlight sliders—for maintaining very bright details without
blowing them out to pure white. If the slider value is decreased (drag to
the right), the brightest tones are made darker while the darkest are made
lighter; the contrast will flatten. If the slider value is increased (drag to the
left), the brightest areas get brighter while the darkest areas get darker.
Typically, small adjustments are best (**Figure 74c**).

Figure 74c A modest decrease in the Gamma value can help to restore extremely
bright highlight details or clipped shadows.

Exposure—Drag this slider to the right to boost the brightness of the overall scene. **Figure 74d** shows the scene has been brightened slightly, while taking the white clouds near the clipping point (this will be handled by the Highlights slider).

Figure 74d The Exposure slider is used to set the global brightness of the scene.

Detail—This slider provides the same functionality as the Clarity slider in the Basic panel of Lightroom and ACR; drag the slider to the right to increase apparent detail and sharpness. If you're working on a subject (like a portrait) that requires smoother texture detail, drag the slider to the left (**Figure 74e**).

Recover Details

Often, if you set the brightness you like and the brightest areas are clipped, you can recover their detail with the Highlights slider.

Figure 74e Use the Detail slider to enhance the perceived sharpness of the image, particularly in the midtone areas.

Shadow—This slider can help to restore detail to the darkest areas of the image without flattening the contrast.

Highlight—This slider allows details in very bright areas to be recovered without flattening the contrast (**Figure 74f**).

Figure 74f The Highlight slider recovers detail in the very brightest areas of the scene without flattening the contrast.

Edge Glow

You may have noticed that many HDR photographs that are posted online and shown elsewhere have an almost illustrative quality to them. For the purpose of this book, the focus will be on keeping things as authentic-looking as possible. The Edge Glow controls allow you to do this.

Radius—This slider controls the size of the glow effect around high-contrast edges.

Strength—This slider determines how pronounced the glow effect is. Using the Radius and Strength sliders requires some experimentation to get a feel for how each setting interacts with the other.

Figure 74g illustrates how the two controls interact for the example daylight scene. The clouds are the focus here because they show the most obvious signs of the glow settings that have been used. Notice that you can blow out the highlights if your combination of settings is too high.

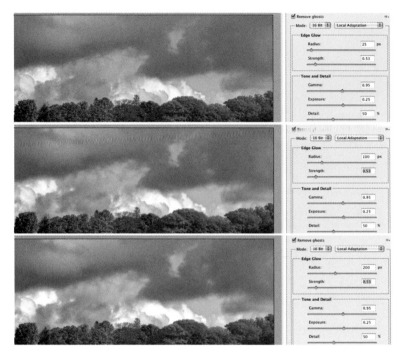

Figure 74g The Edge Glow controls in Merge to HDR Pro allow you to define whether the higher-contrast areas take on a more realistic or surrealistic look.

#**75** HDR Pro: Color and Curves

The final step in perfecting your HDR photo is to enhance the global color values and to fine-tune your global contrast.

Color Panel—This panel uses Vibrance and Saturation controls that work on the same principles as those in the Lightroom Basic panel. Typically, it's best to make smaller adjustments with the Saturation slider and then use the Vibrance slider to finalize the edit (**Figure 75a**).

Reading the Curve/ Histogram

Histograms are an abstract representation of all the tonal data in your image. The left edge of the histogram represents pure black tones (100% gray), the right edge pure white tones (0% gray). The central area represents the midtones (the precise middle represents 50% gray tones). Large "spikes" indicate that a relatively greater proportion of tones from your image lie in that region. Figure 75c indicates most of the data in this HDR image is found in the midtone areas.

Figure 75a The Vibrance and Saturation sliders work in concert to boost the general color intensity of your images.

Point Curves & Corner Points—At first glance, the Merge to HDR Pro Curves panel looks a bit pedestrian. There are no channel controls and no Targeted Adjustment tools. However, the Corner option at the bottom of the panel makes all the difference over a standard curve controller.

To start using the Curve, take a look at your HDR preview and decide if there are localized regions that could be brightened or darkened in isolation, then set points along the curve to divide up the tonal regions (**Figure 75b**).

Curve Pointers

Essentially, there are two reasons to set a point on the curve:

- To adjust the curve and therefore the brightness of that tonal region

- To anchor the curve on the side opposite your adjustments so that those tones are not affected

More on Edge Glow

Even though Edge Glow was handled after the Tone and Detail controls here, it can be useful to go back and check a second time after you've applied your tone curve, because it has a strong effect on contrast. Move the Radius slider back and forth a bit and ensure that you have the look you prefer, then do the same with the Strength slider.

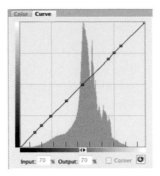

Figure 75b Set the Curve points so that you have one or more control points in the areas you wish to modify, as well as one control point for each area to isolate the edits.

To create your *anchor points*, highlight them one by one, and click the Corner button each time. When that is done, you can start to nudge the other curve points to create the desired contrast. Dragging a point downward will darken the tones; dragging a point upward will brighten the tones (**Figure 75c**). Notice how the Corner points isolate the edits.

Figure 75c Corner points make it easy to isolate curve adjustments.

When you have the look you like, click OK to finalize the HDR merge, and Photoshop will begin processing the data into a 16-bit file.

#76 Photomerge Panoramas

Creating panoramas is one of the more satisfying things you can do with Photoshop. As with HDR, your eyes and mind tend to take in more information and sense a "wider scene" when you look at a beautiful vista in nature, an impressive city skyline, or other wide-open scenes. However, when you try to capture that same scene with a wide-angle lens, something gets "lost in translation" due to the perspective distortions and other issues. You can overcome this problem by taking multiple, overlapping exposures of a wide-angle scene and using Photoshop to seamlessly "stitch" them together.

Shooting Tips for Panoramas

As with HDR photography, there are a few tips to keep in mind.

- Use Aperture Priority mode on your camera. Choose a single aperture using your depth-of-field preview, and, as you move the camera to each new angle of view, focus on a part of the frame that is roughly the same distance away as each previous focal point.

- Use a tripod. It is possible to create great results using a handheld lens with vibration reduction technology, but why take chances?

- Shoot in vertical orientation and overlap each frame you shoot by 20 to 30%. Make sure there are some obvious details in each overlap that are shared by the previous photo so that Photoshop can make sense of the scene and stitch it together with no duplicate or missing features.

Creating the Panorama

After you've taken the overlapping exposures for your panorama, imported them, and processed them in Lightroom or ACR, choose File > Automate > Photomerge. This opens the Photomerge dialog box, which includes the same options as Merge to HDR Pro for selecting files, plus several additional options covered in the following sections (**Figure 76a**).

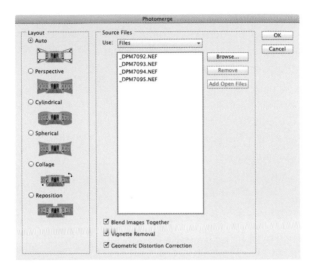

Figure 76a The Photomerge dialog box.

Layout

The options in this section define the algorithms or methods Photoshop uses for stitching your exposures together.

Auto—This method usually produces very good results and is the option I choose most often. Photoshop evaluates your images and chooses to stitch them using a Perspective, Cylindrical, or Spherical layout.

Perspective—This method takes the middle image as a reference image and uses a combination of scale, skew, and rotate transforms on the other files to create a seamless extension.

Cylindrical—This method is for extremely wide-angle panoramas that cannot be processed with the Perspective method.

Spherical—This method works much like Cylindrical except that it's designed for use with 360-degree panoramas.

Collage—This method aligns the layers and uses scale and rotate transforms to match the details.

Reposition—This method aligns the layers but does not use transforms to match the details.

Source File-Handling Options

The Photomerge dialog box also provides a few important options for handling your source.

Blend Images Together—Photoshop attempts to "smooth over" the differences in tone and color so there are no seams. Leave this turned on for all panoramas.

Vignette Removal—This option corrects any overly dark or light edges or corners, so that the exposure appears consistent across the entire scene. I tend to leave this selected as well.

Geometric Distortion Correction—This option removes any obvious barrel distortion or pincushion distortions in the scene. It is recommended you leave this on, unless you already handled geometric distortions in Lightroom or ACR.

The uncropped panorama is shown in **Figure 76b**. Notice how Photoshop has used the four exposures as layers and masked away the extraneous parts after the various transforms and blends were applied.

Figure 76b Photomerge can make quick work of panoramic landscapes and other wide-angle subject matter. Notice the lack of seams.

HDR Panoramas

If you're ambitious, you can create a bracketed exposure of each section of your scene. Then do this:

- Process the shots in Lightroom or ACR for noise reduction and other flaws (see Tip #36).

- Combine each series of exposure values (EV) with Photomerge, using identical settings (that is, if there are EV series of –2, –1, 0, +1, +2, Photomerge all the –2EV shots, then the –1EV shots, and so on).

- Combine the photomerged panoramas in Merge to HDR Pro.

#**77** Spot-Healing Portrait Details

Portrait Retouching Tips

Photoshop offers a wealth of tools and different methods for dealing with common portrait retouching issues like smoothing wrinkle lines, removing blemishes, brightening shadow lines, and sharpening eyes. Photoshop CS5 adds a couple new twists by including a Content-Aware option for the Spot Healing Brush, and by breathing new life into the Sharpen tool. The collection of tips that follows is not exhaustive, but feature the techniques I use most often to get a "quick and clean fix" for portrait retouching.

Note: A pressure-sensitive tablet and stylus are strongly recommended for these edits.

For this image (**Figure 77a**), the faint wrinkle lines around the eyes and the reddish skin on the nose need to be smoothed. You handle these tasks using the Spot Healing Brush (press J or Shift-J to cycle through the group).

Figure 77a Faint wrinkles and minor skin discolorations are easily handled in Photoshop. Here, the unretouched image is shown at 200% magnification. Retouching at 100 to 200% magnification is usually advisable to get the best results.

Once the brush is active, go to the Options bar and under the Brush Picker pop-up, make sure the brush is sized according to the diameter of the wrinkles or blemishes you're attempting to fix. Setting a low-to-medium brush softness and low spacing can also help. Finally, choose the Content-Aware option for the Type of healing, then create a new empty retouching layer(s), and select Sample All Layers in the Options bar (**Figure 77b**). This is a new healing option in Photoshop CS5.

Perfecting Images in Photoshop CS5

Figure 77b Set the Spot Healing Brush Type (or mode) to Content-Aware, then resize the brush so that it is slightly wider than the wrinkle lines you are trying to remove.

Once your brush is set up properly, place the cursor near the start of a wrinkle line and then with one stroke follow the wrinkle to its end and pick up the stylus. Photoshop will immediately use the surrounding texture and color to make a correction (**Figure 77c**).

Figure 77c A quick swipe of the Spot Healing Brush can completely wipe out a wrinkle without leaving any trace.

Next is the spot on the nose. If you try to correct this with the standard Proximity Match mode, you get a bit of a hiccup (**Figure 77d**). Photoshop fixes the color but creates a bright area.

Figure 77d While the Spot Healing Brush's Proximity Match mode works quite well for many uses, it can have a difficult time with relatively high-contrast areas.

Switch back to Content-Aware mode to make the same correction. Not only is the color blemish removed, but the replacement pixels blend very well with the surrounding skin (**Figure 77e**). This figure shows the results of several extra wrinkle-removal passes as well.

Figure 77e Using the Content-Aware heal type with the Spot Healing Brush can quickly yield very smooth and realistic results.

#78 Under-Eye Corrections

Another common retouching task is to lessen the effects of wrinkles or circles directly under the eye. The Spot Healing Brush is again the weapon of choice, using similar settings (and the same retouching layer) as before. Rather than make a single swipe or stroke as when correcting wrinkles, use the Spot Healing Brush to fill the area, taking care not to overlap the eyelid, if you can avoid it (**Figure 78a**).

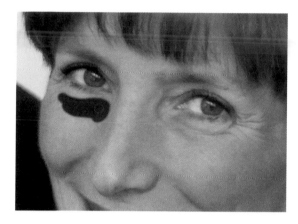

Figure 78a Using the Spot Healing Brush, fill in the area below the eye, taking care not to overlap the eyelid or too much of the surrounding areas.

When you pick up the stylus, you will get a rather fake-looking result (**Figure 78b**), but don't worry, we're not done yet! Tip #79 handles the realism part.

Figure 78b Only halfway there! Use the Spot Healing Brush as the first step in mitigating circles under the eyes.

#79 Enhancing Realism with the Fade Command

Picking up from Tip #78, choose Edit > Fade Spot Healing Brush. This will open the Fade dialog box (**Figure 79**). (If you see something else next to the word Fade, you have made a correction with another tool more recently than the Spot Healing Brush.)

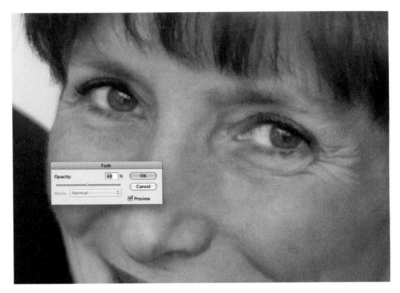

Figure 79 The Fade command dialog box uses a simple percentage slider to help you "throttle back" on the most recent correction.

The purpose of the Fade command here is to "bring back" the original texture, tone, and color underlying the correction and—effectively—mix the two together so that the effect is more natural-looking. This is accomplished by reducing the Opacity value, usually somewhere between 30 and 60%. How much Fade to use is a somewhat subjective judgment.

Note
There cannot be any intermediate steps between the correction you're trying to fade and use of the Fade command itself. You have to use it immediately after the step being faded. Also, if you decide afterward that a different Fade value is required, you cannot step back through history. You will have to remake the correction a second time and Fade it again.

#80 Sharpen Enhancements

For a long time, the Sharpen tool was a bit of an outcast when it came to making quick touch-ups to sharpen details like eyes or other important components of a scene. It was thought to be too blunt an instrument (ironically), often leaving behind artifacts or other unsightly results. No longer! Photoshop CS5 has breathed new life into the Sharpen tool by providing a single, simple setting in the Options bar called Protect Detail (**Figure 80a**).

Figure 80a The Protect Detail option is a new addition to the Sharpen tool that makes it a viable option for quick, local sharpening fixes once again.

Once you try Sharpen with Protect Detail active, you should immediately see a difference in quality between the legacy method of sharpening and the new method. Details are much better preserved, and there are very few artifacts, except occasionally on very high Strength settings. **Figure 80b** is a side-by-side comparison: the left image has no sharpening; the center image has sharpening at 65% with Protect Detail selected; the right image shows sharpening at 65% with no detail protection.

Figure 80b Accurate, quick local sharpening fixes are now possible for small details using the Sharpen tool and the Protect Details option.

#81 Generating Layers from Selections

Even though there is an element of creativity to many of the processes discussed to this point, there are several features in Photoshop (which we will cover in Tips #81 through #84) that take creative editing to the next level. Two are brand new in Photoshop CS5.

The Puppet Warp tool allows you to isolate specific subjects in a scene and then bend and warp them in realistic or otherwise fun ways. The Content-Aware Fill command takes gap filling to a new level, allowing you to fill in the transparent holes caused by other edits with an extremely high degree of realism in most cases. Finally, although the Lens Blur filter is not new for CS5, it nevertheless provides a high degree of precision when it comes to making realistic camera-blur effects in your photos.

The first step in the Puppet Warp workflow is to create a new layer from a carefully selected object in the scene; that layer will be used later as part of the Puppet Warp process. The new layer process also provides the opportunity to create a handy target for the new Content-Aware fill command. Let's take a look. The flag in **Figure 81a** will eventually serve as the "puppet" in Tip #83, but for now it needs to be selected.

Figure 81a This flag will stand in as a "puppet" later in Tip #83.

1. Press W or Shift-W to cycle through the group to choose the Quick Select tool. Set the diameter you are comfortable with (usually somewhere around 60 pixels is a good starting point so that the brush can fit in tight spaces) and make the selection by dragging across your subject.

2. Zoom in to the selection to be sure you haven't missed any spots or added something that doesn't belong. If you need to add something, make a very short brushstroke over the missed area. If you need to remove something, press and hold the Alt key and drag a short brushstroke over that area (**Figure 81b**).

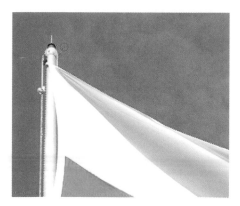

Figure 81b To remove the sections erroneously included in the selection, press and hold the Alt key and make short brushstrokes over areas in the background. To add to a selection, just make additional short brushstrokes (no modifier key required).

3. Click the Refine Edge button on the Options bar. Use the Smart Radius and Color enhancement techniques discussed in Tips #65 and #66 to refine your selection.

4. Make sure to double-click your selection layer if it's a background (to create transparency behind it), then choose Layer > New > Layer via Cut, or Shift-Command-J (Mac OS) or Shift-Control-J (Windows). This cuts and pastes the selected subject onto a new layer, leaving it in place. When the new layer's visibility is off, the transparent hole in the original is visible (**Figure 81c**).

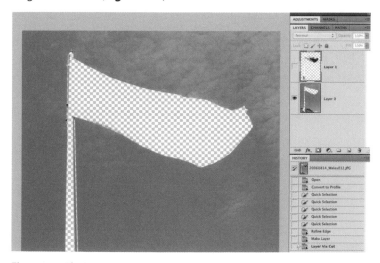

Figure 81c The New Layer Via Cut command is a good way to isolate your subject from the rest of the image, preparing it for an eventual Puppet Warp workflow.

#**82** Using Content-Aware Fill

Now let's take a look at Photoshop CS5's new ability to accurately fill transparent holes (or holes with empty pixels) in a layer. This is achieved using the Content-Aware Fill command. Here are the basic steps:

1. Select the layer with the empty or transparent pixels in the Layers panel and make a Lasso selection (press L or Shift-L to cycle through the group) around a portion of it. Content-Aware Fill usually produces the best results when you break an empty area into 4 to 6 pieces and correct them individually.

2. Choose Edit > Fill to invoke the Fill dialog box (**Figure 82a**). Under the Contents section choose Content-Aware from the Use pop-up menu. Leave the Mode set to Normal, the Opacity set to 100%, and the Preserve Transparency option deselected.

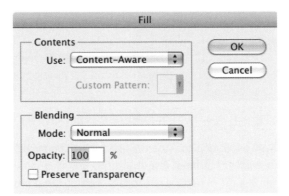

Figure 82a The Fill dialog box provides options for choosing the method and Blending Mode for any selection fill. Choose Content-Aware and leave the Blending options at their default settings.

3. Click OK and Photoshop will intelligently guess what type of texture and content belong in the selection area (**Figure 82b**). Repeat this process as many times as necessary to fill the entire gap. Filling gaps in this way allows you to achieve more natural-looking results when your new layer is warped.

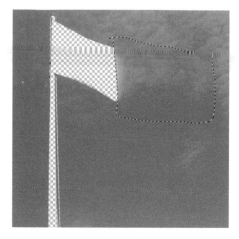

Figure 82b Content-Aware Fill does a remarkable job of "guessing what belongs" in the gaps that you attempt to fill with it. If you don't get a nearly perfect result the first try, Undo and repeat the command; there is an element of randomness to its results.

#83 Getting Creative with Puppet Warp

Once your subject is isolated and you have filled the transparent hole it left behind, you can try your hand at being a digital puppeteer. Turn on the visibility of the new layer you created in Tip #81; the image should look as it did when you started. Choose Edit > Puppet Warp. This is also a new feature in Photoshop CS5. A special grid will display over your layer and provide several settings in the Options bar (**Figure 83a**).

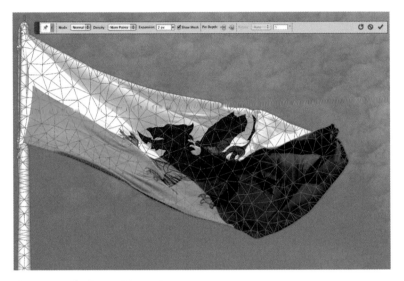

Figure 83a The Puppet Warp options.

Mode Menu

There are three different types of warping that Photoshop can apply: Rigid, Normal, and Distort. These refer to the amount of elasticity applied to your subject when warping. Generally, Normal will strike a good balance between texture quality and warp flexibility.

Density Menu

Density refers to the number of triangles that make up the grid or mesh that covers your warp subject. The higher the density, the smoother the results of the warp but the longer the processing time. Generally, the Normal density works well.

(Mesh) Expansion

This setting expands or contracts the outer edge of the grid or mesh.

Pins and Pin Depth

Pins are the small markers along your warp layer that Photoshop uses to warp the image when you click and drag them.

Pins— This method allows you to push, pull, bend, or rotate part of the mesh, and therefore the layer that is attached to the mesh. To add a pin, click the spot on the mesh where you want the pin to be located. When you select a pin, it displays a black dot in the middle; a selected pin is also known as the *active pin*, .

To move part of the mesh, click a pin and drag. To rotate the mesh instead of dragging it, select the pin and press and hold the Alt key. A small circle will appear around the pin; drag it to rotate. **Figure 83b** shows several pins attached to the mesh, with the active pin being rotated. To delete a pin, right-click it and choose Delete Pin from the context menu. To delete all pins and start over, click the Remove All Pins button on the Options Bar, .

Figure 83b The ability to manipulate pins allows you to generate the warped layer mesh.

Pin Depth—This setting is useful when you wrap part of the grid or mesh over on itself (overlap areas controlled by other pins), and need to reveal a portion of the mesh that is hidden from view. As you click the Set Pin Forward (Left) and Set Pin Backward (Right) buttons,  different areas of the overlapping mesh will be "pulled to the top."

Essentially, the overlapping areas are treated like stacked layers. Clicking the Set Pin Forward and Set Pin Backward buttons reveals different parts of the "stack." The trick is to remember that you are not changing the order of the pins; rather, you're changing which part of the overlapping meshes are "attached" to the active pin and therefore, which part of the mesh will move when you move that pin (**Figure 83c**).

Figure 83c Use the Set Pin Forward and Set Pin Backward buttons to change which portion of an overlapping mesh is attached to the active pin.

Rotate

This setting determines whether a pin will be automatically rotated based on the warp mode and other settings (Auto), or whether it will rotate a fixed number of degrees (Fixed). Generally, leaving this to Auto works well. If you want to use Fixed, choose it from the Rotate pop-up menu and in the text field to the right, type in the number of degrees.

The Finished Warp

Figure 83d shows the final warp arrangement with all mesh settings and pins visible; **Figure 83e** shows the final image with warps applied.

More on Puppet Warp

Because it is a somewhat complex process, you can view a video of the Puppet Warp tool in action on this book's product page at Peachpit.com.

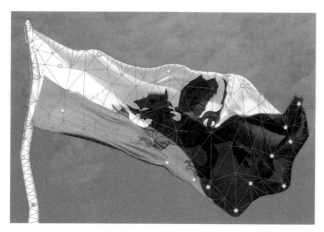

Figure 83d Very complex warps can be set up using the Normal Mode and Mesh Density.

Figure 83e The final warped flag.

#84 Softening Focus with the Lens Blur Filter

Many times, photographers may find themselves evaluating a shot that they feel has positive qualities, but because of the aperture and distances used in the shot, the background remains too much in focus (**Figure 84a**). This usually has the effect of drawing the viewer's eye away from the intended focal point. All is not lost in this case; the Lens Blur filter is designed to apply an authentic-looking blur to specific areas of an image, while leaving other areas unaffected.

Figure 84a The shot of this abandoned park bench is interesting, but the background was left too much in focus, thereby detracting from the quality of the shot.

Setup
Decide which portions of the image need to be protected from the blur.

1. Make a selection around that area. Since you don't need to precisely outline the edges of your subject, use the Lasso tool (press L or Shift L to cycle through the group) and make a relatively smooth outline around the subject; avoid creating any harsh angles.

2. Use Refine Edge (Command-Alt-R for Mac OS or Control-Alt-R for Windows) to add several pixels of feathering. This will smooth the contour of the selection; you may also need to expand the selection slightly (**Figure 84b**).

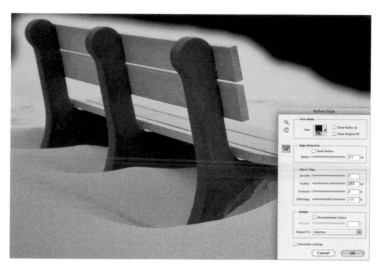

Figure 84b Use the Refine Edge command to smooth the transition of the selection area; this helps to avoid an obvious boundary between the areas of focus and blur.

3. Create an alpha channel for your selection.

4. Go to the Layers panel and make sure your target layer is selected before choosing Filter > Blur > Lens Blur. This opens the image in the Lens Blur dialog box (**Figure 84c**).

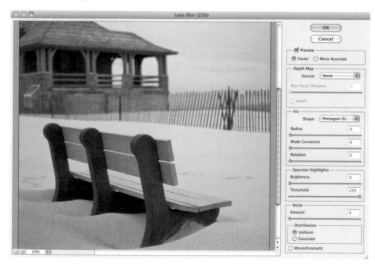

Figure 84c The Lens Blur filter.

Preview

These settings control whether the blur preview is turned on as you make your changes, and whether the preview errs toward speed or quality. The Lens Blur Filter is hardware-intensive. Typically, leaving Preview selected and set to Faster provides an adequate quality preview.

Depth Map

Make sure your alpha channel is selected (it should be by default); this is the means through which Photoshop can avoid blurring your in-focus subjects (**Figure 84d**). If you prefer, you can create a layer mask from the selection and choose that from the Source menu. With the Source chosen, move the cursor over the image preview (look for a crosshair), then click a part of the image you want blurred. The slider should move, and you may see some blurring right away.

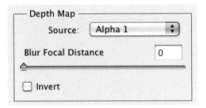

Figure 84d Make sure to choose the alpha channel or layer mask that was generated from the original selection so Photoshop has a reference for protecting the in-focus areas.

Iris

The Iris settings contain four controls that are analogs to the physical characteristics of a camera lens. They are shown in **Figure 84e**.

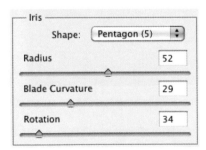

Figure 84e The Lens Blur Iris settings mimic the physical properties of camera lenses and create the blur effect being applied to the image.

Shape—This pop-up menu provides six options for defining the shape of the lens iris that is being simulated. Without getting too technical, traditional camera lenses have a series of interwoven, mechanical "leaves" that move together to create the aperture opening for the lens. This is called the Iris and is analogous to the human eye where the Iris adjusts on the fly, to expand or reduce the size of the pupil, letting in more or less light. Generally, the lower the number of sides, the less blur is perceived between contrast edges in the photo; the effect can be very subtle between one option and the next.

Radius—This setting sets the strength of the lens-blur effect and relates to the hole created by a lens Iris (better known as the lens' *aperture*).

Blade Curvature—This setting defines how rounded the aperture opening is; the higher the value, the more high contrast the edge details become blurred. The effects of this slider are quite subtle and usually require a magnification of at least 50% or 100% to be noticed.

Rotate—This setting defines the amount of rotation for the Iris. The Rotate effect is even more subtle than Blade Curvature, but the best generalization is that it seems to slightly lighten or darken low-contrast edge details.

Specular Highlights

If there are very bright areas in your scene, some of that brightness may be lost initially as you create the blur. To "restore" the specular brightness, move the Brightness slider to the right. To decide what portion of the tonal range should be affected, drag the Threshold setting to the left. Generally, small changes to both are more than enough.

Noise

The Noise sliders in the Lens Blur filter can add some "grit" to the blurred areas in your scene. They can also prevent a blurred image from looking "smoothed over." You can choose: an Amount; whether the noise is uniformly distributed or not; and whether it's monochromatic (recommended). If used at all, these settings are best used sparingly. Amount values over 5 or 6 can quickly create an unpleasant effect. The final results of the Lens Blur session for the bench are in **Figure 84f**. No Noise or Specular settings were used in this case.

Figure 84f The final composition is more effective because the background is now blurred in a way that doesn't pull the viewer's eye away from the bench and footprints.

#85 Introducing Bristle Tips

Photoshop CS5 provides two excellent painting enhancements: Bristle Tips and the new Mixer Brush. We'll focus on the former in this tip, then the Mixer Brush workflow in the next tip. Bristle Tips offer two primary advantages:

- They provide a realistic simulation of real paintbrush behaviors.

- Bristle Tip behaviors can be previewed as you paint with it.

Getting Started

Bristle Tips brushes are easily identified in the Brush panel and Brush Preset Pickers by the detailed icons they use (see the "Bristle Tips" sidebar). There are two primary types (or shapes) of Bristle Tip presets, and five sub-types for each, although you can customize them and create your own presets.

Once a brush tool is selected and one of the Bristle Tips presets chosen, open the Brush panel and have a look at the unique parameters, including: bristle shape; number of bristles (Bristles slider), bristle length, bristle thickness, bristle stiffness, bristle angle, and Spacing. **Figure 85a** shows the Bristle Tips "Qualities" settings.

Figure 85a Bristle Tips Qualities and Preview as seen in the Brush panel.

Bristle Tips

Each bristle tip is shown with the icon it uses in the Brush panel and Brush Preset Pickers (in the Options bar):

Rounded Shape
- Round Point
- Round Blunt
- Round Curve
- Round Angle
- Round Fan

Flat Shape
- Flat Point
- Flat Blunt
- Flat Curve
- Flat Angle
- Flat Fan

Painting

If you plan to do extensive photo-painting or other creative painting workflows, you can set up the Photoshop workspace for that purpose. Click the Painting button in the App bar,

ESSENTIALS   DESIGN   **PAINTING**   PHOTOGRAPHY   »

Alternatively, choose Window > Workspace > Painting. This workspace will include several panels useful to painting workflows, including the Brush panel, Brush Presets panel, the Swatches panel, as well as several others.

OpenGL

Several of the new features in Photoshop CS5 and CS5 Extended require an OpenGL compatible GPU (or graphics card) to simulate 3D objects. The Bristle Brush Preview is one such feature. Choose Help > Photoshop Help and search "OpenGL" to find out more about which features use this technology and which graphics cards are supported.

Once you find a series of settings that you like, you can save Bristle Tips as custom presets by using the Brush panel flyout menu, choosing New Brush Preset, naming the preset, and clicking OK in the Brush Name dialog box.

Previewing

Photoshop CS5 provides a floating overlay called the Bristle Brush Preview (requires a graphics card that supports OpenGL information) that sits atop the active document when activated. You can turn it on by clicking the left-most icon at the very bottom of the Brush panel. From that point, you can click its header and drag it to move the preview to any portion of your window. As you move the stylus in different ways, the preview provides real-time feedback for the brush's tilt angle, barrel rotation (requires Wacom 6D Art Pen), and the amount of pressure being placed on the brush tip. By default, the Bristle Brush Preview shows a grayscale brush, but if you press and hold the Shift key and click the overlay, a rendered 3D preview appears (**Figure 85b**).

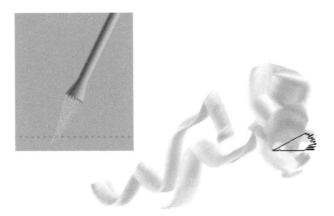

Figure 85b You can preview the Bristle Tips as you move the stylus, as a means of getting used to the tool and providing some visual feedback.

Experimenting

The best way become familiar with each Bristle Tip and setting is to turn on the Bristle Brush Preview and try them out on a few throwaway photos. Notice what happens as you change directions mid-stroke, tilt the stylus, and rotate it in different ways.

#**86** Using the Mixer Brush

Hopefully, you now have a better understanding of how Bristle Tips differ from normal brush presets, but it's important to look at the other side of the equation. The Mixer Brush goes a long way toward achieving many of the painting effects that can be created in programs like Corel Painter, but with a fraction of the learning curve. The secret of the Mixer Brush is that it treats color pixels like real paint; this means that you can blend colors in new ways and create new kinds of brushstrokes that previously were not possible.

To access the Mixer Brush (which shares a group with the standard Brush tool), press B or Shift-B to cycle through the group. The Mixer Brush icon displays a small paint droplet with a brush, ✔. When you select the Mixer Brush, the Options bar populates with sever al settings for controlling the "digital paint" in your photo (**Figure 86a**). The most important settings for getting started are described in more detail in the following sections.

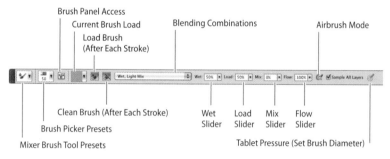

Figure 86a   The new Mixer Brush settings in the Options bar.

Brush Loading

This setting mimics the process of paint accumulating among the bristles and on the surface of a paintbrush. To use brush loading, click the Load Brush button on the Options bar, and increase the Load slider value before you paint.

As a photographer, when painting over photos, I prefer not to load the brush so that as I paint a specific area of detail, only the colors from that area are mixed and moved on the canvas. This is of course a subjective decision; like real painting, there are no strict rules.

Brush Cleaning

Photoshop offers the option to clean off the digitally simulated paintbrush each time you pick up the stylus. To clean the brush after each stroke, click the Clean Brush button. To create a more organic-looking painting or if you're painting to an empty canvas, you may want to leave this setting off and clean the brush manually by opening the Current Brush Load pop-up and choosing Clean Brush (**Figure 86b**).

Figure 86b The Current Brush Load pop-up menu provides options for manually cleaning and loading the brush as you paint.

Wet

The Wet setting describes the *viscosity* or "wetness" of the digital pixels that you'll be spreading across the canvas. Like real paintings, the less dry the paint is, the more it can be spread across the canvas, mixing with other colors and textures as you do so. **Figure 86c** shows brushstrokes that use (from left to right) a Wet value of 10%, 50%, and 100%. The Bristle Tip settings and all other Mixer Brush settings were the same.

Figure 86c The Wet slider helps to set up the characteristic of the simulated paint, whether it is dry or very wet, allowing the pixels to spread and mix colors more easily.

Mix

This setting defines the mix ratio or the tendency of the colors on the canvas to mix together as you brush over them, creating new colors. When using real paints, certain types mix to create new colors, while others tend to cover up underlying colors, depending on the mediums used and other variables. **Figure 86d** shows brushstrokes that use (from top to bottom) a Mix value of 0%, 40%, and 80%. All other settings were the same.

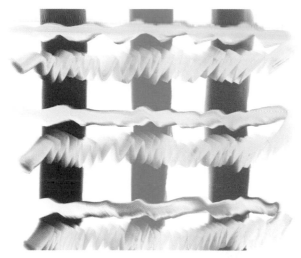

Figure 86d The Mix slider helps to define the amount of color mixing that occurs as you move your brush across the image.

Flow

The Flow defines the amount or "density" of the simulated paint that's being put down on the canvas. The higher the value, the denser the paint will be, and the colors and details underneath will show through less.

Start Painting

The easiest way to get started with the Mixer Brush is to click the Useful Combinations pop-up menu (**Figure 86e**). It combines four paint states (Dry, Moist, Wet, and Very Wet) with three levels of paint loading or mixing (Medium, Light, and Heavy). The Medium Mix options are the first in each series.

Figure 86e The Blending Combinations pop-up menu makes it very easy to begin experimenting with the Mixer brush and understanding how it uses the Wet, Mix, and Load values to simulate paint being spread across a canvas.

For photo-painting, my usual process is to create an empty layer over the Background (so I'm not painting on the original). Make sure the Sample All Layers option is turned on. Then I use either the Moist or Wet presets, with either normal or heavy mix settings. From there, I use a smaller, more fine-tipped brush and short brushstrokes that make it easy to follow the contours of fine details, while using broader brush tips and longer strokes when working with large areas of homogenous texture like skies or water (**Figure 86f**).

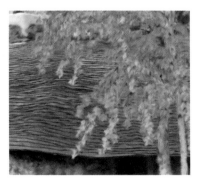

Figure 86f Examples of painterly effects that can be achieved with the Bristle Tips and Mixer Brush.

#**87** HDR Toning

The HDR Toning (**Figure 87a**) adjustment is designed to create photographs that take on an HDR-like appearance, using the controls similar to those found in Merge to HDR Pro. You can use HDR Toning on either a single exposure, or as an extension of Merge to HDR Pro.

For individual images, choose Image > Adjustments > HDR Toning. The HDR Toning controls will look very familiar to you if you've already spent time working with Merge to HDR Pro. Each of the controls, including the Curves and Corner points, works in exactly the same way as they do in Merge to HDR Pro (see Tips #72 through 75 for more details).

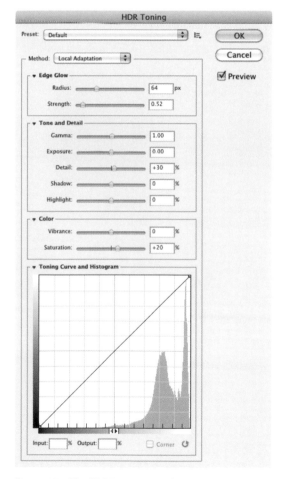

Figure 87a The HDR Toning controls.

Image Adjustments

This section includes the last of the retouching and image-enhancement tips, and it focuses on one of the most important (if not *the* most important) areas in Photoshop. Image Adjustments are the tools of choice for precisely handling colors, tones, and contrast in a photograph, as well as some of the most powerful and useful photo-styling tools. We'll wrap up the section with a *pseudo adjustment*—the new Neutral Density preset for the Gradient tool.

32-Bit HDR Toning

To use the HDR Toning Adjustment as a tool for editing 32-bit HDR files, open your exposures into Merge to HDR Pro, choosing the 32-bit mode, then set the white point with the slider. From this point you can open the image into Photoshop to apply the HDR Toning controls.

Some important items to remember with HDR Toning:

- The image will only be as good as the base exposure, so the best bet is to start with a well-exposed raw or DNG file that has plenty of detail in the highlights and shadows, as well as the midtone areas.

- Unlike most Image Adjustments, there is no adjustment layer for HDR Toning, and HDR Toning cannot be used as a Smart Filter to create nondestructive edits. It requires a flattened file.

- If you're going for a stylized look, try the Photorealistic High Contrast option in the Preset pop-up and tweak any settings that have created problems with overdone details or details lost in the highlight areas. **Figure 87b** shows a scene that uses this technique, with settings

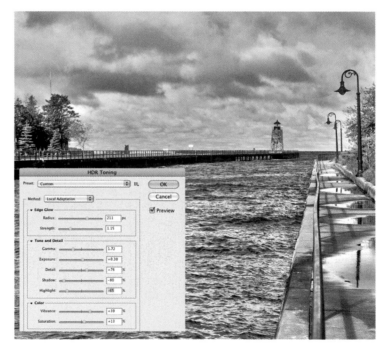

Figure 87b The HDR Toning Presets can provide a useful shortcut for creating stylized HDR.

#**88** Shadows/Highlights

The Shadows/Highlights adjustment is one of the more powerful and precise ways to improve the global contrast in your photos. It is most commonly used to enhance flat or washed-out exposures where the highlights may need to be darkened a bit and the shadows brightened to reveal their detail and color. Essentially, Shadows/Highlights can achieve many of the same effects that a Curves adjustment can but uses a more intuitive process. **Figure 88a** shows a photo with a relatively flat contrast in the shadows and darker midtone areas.

Figure 88a The Shadows/Highlights adjustment can be used to improve shots like this that have been processed in ACR or Lightroom but need localized contrast.

To access the Shadows/Highlights adjustment, choose Image > Adjustment > Shadows/Highlights. You may notice an immediate improvement to the overall contrast and details visible in the darker parts of the image (**Figure 88b**). If you have used Shadows/Highlights before, it is worth noting that Adobe has reduced the default shadow boost in Photoshop CS5 so that fewer tweaks are needed to achieve a good result. This setting and others are described in the following sections.

Figure 88b The simple act of opening the Shadows/Highlights adjustment will have an immediate positive impact on your photo. Adobe has decreased the default Shadow adjustment amount as well to reduce the number of steps required.

Shadows

The three settings at the top of the dialog box control the degree to which the shadow details are given a "brightness boost," or in some cases the degree to which they will be made darker. **Figure 88c** shows the shadow correction based on the Amount, Tonal Width, and Radius settings.

Amount—This slider controls the strength or intensity of the shadow boost.

Tonal Width—This slider defines the scope of the shadow correction. Higher values will include some midtones as well as shadows and will therefore cause more of the image to be brightened or darkened.

Radius—This slider defines the local contrast in the areas that are being brightened or darkened. Higher values will result in higher contrast.

Figure 88c The first step in a Shadows/Highlights session is to define the amount of shadow area to be affected (Tonal Width), the intensity (Amount) of the effect, and the final contrast (Radius).

Highlights

The Highlights settings operate on the exact same principle as the Shadows settings, except that you're controlling the look of the brighter portions of the image rather than the darker portions. When the two corrections are combined, they can create a more dramatic and interesting contrast, as well as reveal detail. **Figure 88d** shows the results of the combined correction. Compare the tree-line area as well as the sky in this shot to Figure 88a.

Figure 88d The second step to creating a more pleasing global contrast and detail in your image is to define the Highlight areas. In this case, Shadows settings were used to brighten up the tree line, while Highlights settings were used to darken up the sky and add contrast to the clouds.

Adjustments

The bottom of the dialog box provides four additional controls for tweaking the colors and contrast in your corrected photographs. **Figure 88e** shows the final correction with all settings applied (Color Correction +34; Midtone Contrast +28); compare to Figure 88a.

Color Correction—This slider enhances the intensity of the colors in the areas that have been corrected. This slider works much like the Vibrance slider in Lightroom or ACR (See Tip #25) to reduce or boost the color saturation in a subtle way.

Midtone Contrast—This slider increases or decreases the contrast in the areas of the image that were not corrected.

Black Clip / White Clip—This slider defines the values for how much of the Shadows and Highlights (by percentage) will be clipped to pure black or pure white. I generally do not change these settings, preferring to instead set that value with the Curves dialog box if necessary.

Figure 88e The final correction from the Shadows/Highlights adjustment.

Nondestructive Shadows/Highlights

To use Shadows/Highlights as a Smart Filter, create a copy of the layer you wish to adjust, right-click and choose Convert to Smart Object. Access Shadows/Highlights as you normally would. When finished, click OK and the correction will show up as a Smart Filter (**Figure 88f**).

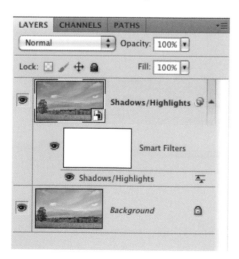

Figure 88f Convert your target layer to a Smart Object before accessing the Shadows/Highlights command.

#89 Using Adjustment Layers

When working with Image Adjustments, there are two ways to apply settings to a photograph. You can access them directly from the Image menu and apply the adjustments directly to the pixels in the active layer. This will permanently alter the pixel values when you save the file.

The alternative is to use adjustment layers. Adjustment layers use the same settings and presets, but because they are self-contained, they apply edits nondestructively. There is no permanent change made to the pixels until the layers are merged or flattened. There are three ways to access adjustment layers:

- Choose Layer > New Adjustment Layer and the specific adjustment.

- Click and hold the pop-up menu at the bottom of the Layers panel (fourth icon from left), , and choose your adjustment.

- Click the individual adjustment icons in the Adjustments panel **(Figure 89a)**.

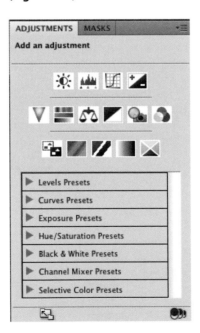

Figure 89a The Photoshop CS5 Adjustments Panel displays icons for each adjustment. Top row: Brightness/Contrast, Levels, Curves, and Exposure. Middle Row: Vibrance, Hue & Saturation, Color Balance, Black & White, Photo Filter, and Channel Mixer. Bottom Row: Invert, Posterize, Threshold, Gradient Map, and Selective Color.

There are fifteen adjustments that have adjustment-layer equivalents; all of them provide the same controls and quality as their cousins from the Image menu. Among the three methods, the quickest way to create an adjustment layer is to click its icon in the Adjustments panel. When an icon is clicked, the image adjustment's controls open inside the Adjustments panel, and a new adjustment layer with a layer mask appears in the Layers panel. **Figure 89b** shows the Curves adjustment and accompanying layer.

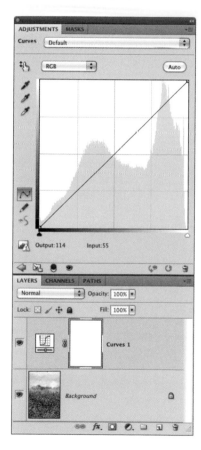

Figure 89b A Newly created Curves adjustment layer as seen in the Adjustments and Layers panels. You can add as many adjustment layers to your document as needed.

Clipping Adjustment Layers

One of the most useful adjustment layer features is the ability to "clip itself" to a single, pixel-based layer so that its settings affect only that layer

Sticking Clippings

You can make the Clip to Layer function "sticky" (that is, the default behavior) by clicking it before you open any adjustment layers.

and none of the other layers in the Layers panel. To use this feature, select the layer that requires adjustment, create the adjustment layer, and click the Clip to Layer button at the bottom of the Adjustments panel (third from left), . The adjustment layer (in the Layers panel) will shift to the right slightly and display a small downward-facing arrow to indicate that the adjustment is clipped to the layer beneath it (**Figure 89c**).

Figure 89c Where adjustment layers are concerned, clipping can be a great help in isolating adjustments to one specific layer.

#90 Targeted Curves Adjustment

The value of using the Tone Curve panel in Lightroom 3 to create targeted adjustments by working directly on the image preview was covered in Tip #26. However, for non-raw photographs or occasions when you need to apply tone-curve edits using Photoshop CS5, the Curves adjustment layer can supply the same solution. To create a targeted curves correction, open a Curves adjustment layer from the Adjustments panel (second from right, top row of icons), then click the Targeted Adjustment icon, .

When the cursor is moved over the document, an eyedropper is displayed. Use this cursor to target the specific tones (for example, bright highlights) that you want to edit with the Curves adjustment, then drag downward to darken those tones, or upward to brighten them. The cursor will change to a hand and arrow, a point will automatically be placed on the curve, and an edit made as you do so (**Figure 90a**). This method is more efficient and in many cases more accurate than manually placing and moving points on the curve.

Figure 90a Use the Curves' targeted adjustment tool to drag directly on the document to set curve points and adjust their position on the curve.

Repeat the eyedropper process with as many tonal regions on the document as needed; new points will be placed on the curve as you do so. This same process can be applied individually to the red, green, or blue channel data in a photo by using the Channel pop-up menu, . This is quite useful when you have a color cast that makes the image too warm, greenish/yellowish, or cool, respectively.

When you're finished using the Curves adjustment, click the pixel-based layer you want to modify next, and the Adjustments panel will return to its default state so that you can add more adjustments as needed. **Figure 90b** depicts a split image showing the before (left) and after (right) for this adjustment.

Figure 90b The Curves adjustment, when combined with the Shadows/Highlights adjustment, provides a very powerful solution for improving the global and localized areas of contrast in your scene.

#91 Localized Color Vibrance

The Vibrance adjustment layer applies the same effect as the Vibrance sliders found in Lightroom and ACR (see Tip #26) and offers two controls: one for enhancing color saturation with Vibrance and one for Saturation.

1. Open the Vibrance adjustment in the Adjustments panel (left-most icon, second row), then set up the colors to suit your taste, using smaller values for Saturation and larger ones for Vibrance (**Figure 91a**).

Figure 91a The Vibrance adjustment layer is a great way to further enhance the color intensity of your photography.

To isolate the Vibrance adjustments to select parts of the image, use the Masks panel to rapidly set up a layer.

2. Select the layer mask in the Vibrance adjustment layer (looks like an empty white box), open the Masks panel, and click the Color Range button. The Color Range dialog box will appear over your image.

(continued on next page)

3. As described in Tip #62, choose the Image preview in the dialog box and set the Selection Preview to Black Matte or White Matte, depending on whether your subjects are lighter or darker.

4. Click the Localized Color Clusters option and set the fuzziness somewhere between 50 and 100 to start.

5. Use the eyedropper to click an area on the Color Range preview that you want adjusted. Shift-click more areas to include those. As you do so, more and more of your image should become visible (**Figure 91b**).

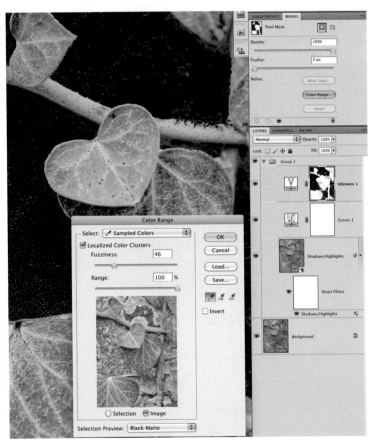

Figure 91b Using the Masks panel and the Color Range command you can quickly set up a color selection that will generate a precise mask when finished.

6. When you're finished, click OK and Photoshop will generate a precise layer mask based on your Color Range settings, allowing the Vibrance adjustment to show through in only selected areas (**Figure 91c**).

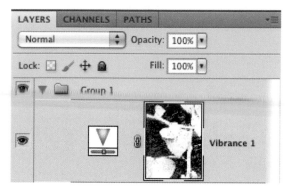

Figure 91c A Vibrance adjustment was combined with a layer mask.

#92 Black and White Styling

Creating black-and-white photos is easy with the Black & White adjustment layer in Photoshop CS5.

1. Open a Black & White adjustment layer from the Adjustments panel (third icon from the right, second row) (**Figure 92a**).

Figure 92a The Black & White adjustment panel, seen with the default settings.

2. Click the Targeted Adjustment icon and move the cursor over the document. As you do so, you will see that this targeted adjustment uses the same cursors as those described in Tip #90, while it uses controls that behave similarly to the Black & White controls discussed in Tip #30. When you click on the photo and drag left, Photoshop will darken any tones that contain that color (from the original). Click and drag right to brighten all the areas that contain a color.

3. (Optional) If you would like to tint your black-and-white image to give it a classic look such as Sepia Tone or Cyanotype, select the Tint check box and click the color well next to it, , to open Photoshop's Color Picker. From that point, the color you pick will be previewed automatically in the background so you can see the effect.

4. (Optional) If you would like to create an Infrared-styled black-and-white photo, click the Black & White presets pop-up menu and choose Infrared, ![] . The result of that styling can be seen in **Figure 92b**.

Figure 92b A photograph that has been converted to an Infrared black-and-white photo using the Black & White adjustment panel.

#93 Photo Filters

Photoshop also has a collection of digital "filters" that simulate the glass kind and which can be applied as an adjustment layer.

1. Open a Photo Filter adjustment from the Adjustments panel (second icon from the right, second row). **Figure 93a** shows a cluster of wine grapes and vine leaves that could stand to be warmed up to simulate warmer light. By default, the Warming Filter (85) is preview; however, the preview is off in this case to show the original image.

Figure 93a Photos that are slightly too cool-colored or warm-colored because of the light they were shot in can be tweaked using a Photo Filter adjustment.

2. To simulate a classic filter type, select the Filter mode, choose a filter type from the pop-up, and adjust the Density slider to increase or decrease the intensity of the effect (**Figure 93b**).

Figure 93b The Photo Filter image adjustment contains several presets that mimic the effects of real-world color filters.

3. To set up a filter that mimics a color found in your scene, select the Color mode and click the color well to open the Color Picker.

4. Move the cursor over your document preview to display an eyedropper, then press and hold the Command key (Mac OS) or Control key (Windows), and click the color in your image that will be the basis of your filter. Again, set the Intensity to suit your taste. Typically, values between 15% and 35% provide a nice balance (**Figure 93c**).

(continued on next page)

Figure 93c The final image with a custom warming filter applied at 31%.

    Perfecting Images in Photoshop CS5

#94 Organizing and Previewing Multiple Adjustments

One thing about adjustment layers that you have to watch out for is that they can really add up quickly. Luckily, the Layers panel provides a very simple means of grouping and previewing adjustment layers together.

1. Press and hold the Shift key and click each of the adjustment layers in the Layers panel. If you have multiple image layers that are placed between a series of adjustments, handle those adjustments separately.

2. For each group of selected adjustment layers, click under one of their icons while still holding down the Shift key, drag them to the Folder icon (third from the right), at the bottom of the Layers panel, and then release. This creates a new folder called Group 1 and places the adjustment layers inside (**Figure 94**).

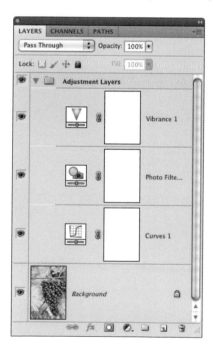

Figure 94 Grouping adjustment layers is a simple task with the Layers panel.

3. Click the folder label to rename it and then press the Return key to accept it. At this point your adjustments are organized so that they can be hidden or viewed together in the Layers panel.

#95 Gradients: Neutral Density

While it's not an adjustment layer or smart filter, there is a preset for the Gradient tool that mimics the effect of a split neutral-density filter. This filter is most commonly used in daylight photography scenes where the sky is far too bright, but the foreground is reasonably well lit. Essentially, the top half of the filter is very dark while the bottom half is clear glass; the end result is that the sky is darkened down in the exposure without affecting the foreground.

1. Press G (or Shift-G) to select the Gradient tool.

2. In the Options bar, click the Gradient Picker, click the flyout menu, and choose Small List or Large List so that you can read the names of the gradient presets (**Figure 95a**).

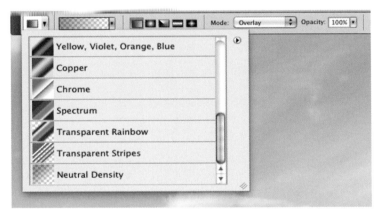

Figure 95a Use the Gradient Picker in the Options bar to choose the Neutral Density gradient preset.

3. Choose Neutral Density.

4. From the Options bar, choose Overlay from the Mode pop-up menu. (I have found this to be very helpful when dealing with skies that are too bright.) If the Overlay mode doesn't work for your purposes, leave the mode set to Normal and try reducing the Opacity between 30% and 50%, depending on the scene. You may need to experiment.

5. Press F to jump to Full Screen with Menu bar mode, then reduce the magnification of your file (Command- for Mac OS or Control- for Windows) so that you can see the entire image and have some room around the edges.

6. Place the Gradient crosshair slightly above the top of your image, drag until the cursor reaches a point in the image that's not too bright, then release (**Figure 95b**). The final result can be seen in **Figure 95c**. Note the difference in the sky's tone and color.

Figure 95b Drag the gradient line down to the point where you want the image to remain bright and then release. If you have an evenly lit sky (from side to side), you can press and hold the Shift key as you do so. For skies that are slightly darker on one side or the other, try to match the angle.

Figure 95c The Neutral Density Gradient preset is a great way to handle skies that are overexposed.

#96 Creating Text on a Path

The ability to create text that follows along a contour in one of your photos (perhaps for a newsletter or other design project) can add a touch of flair and a professional look. The first step to creating text on a path is to create the path with the Pen tool, which works like the other Bezier tools found throughout the Adobe Creative Suite.

Text and Output Tips

Invariably, even if you're not a graphic designer, web designer, or otherwise expect to be heavily involved in the use of text in Photoshop... there *will* be times when it will be useful to know how to use Photoshop's text tools and features. Perhaps you need to make some FPO (For Placement Only) markings for a magazine editor, a small watermark, or even create a quick newsletter for your clients. All these things can be done with the text tools in Photoshop. Similarly, we all need to print and/or move smaller versions of our files to the web, so this section also includes a couple of important tips for working with the Photoshop CS5 Print dialog box and the Save for Web & Devices function.

1. Once a path is created, select the Horizontal Type tool by pressing T (or Shift-T to cycle through the group).

2. Move the text cursor over the edge of the path; the cursor should change, .

3. Click the path where you would like the text to begin.

4. Begin typing your text. When you're finished, resize the text, if necessary, using the Font Size field, , in the Options bar. Text options and the finished text on a path are shown in **Figure 96**.

Figure 96 Adding text to a path is quite easy in Photoshop.

5. (Optional) Open the Character panel (Window > Character), then use the Tracking pop-up menu, , to modify the distances between individual letters.

Perfecting Images in Photoshop CS5

#97 Layer Styles: Drop Shadows

Sometimes the addition of a drop shadow can help that text to stand out against the details and colors in your picture.

1. Highlight the text layer that needs a drop shadow applied, and then from the bottom of the Layers panel, click and hold the Layer Effects button, (second from left), and choose Drop Shadow (**Figure 97a**).

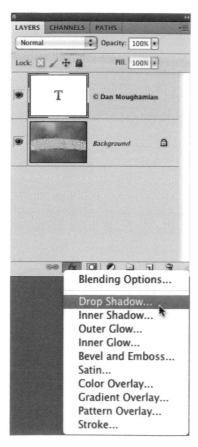

Figure 97a The different layer effects (or Layer Styles) available from the Fx pop-up menu at the bottom of the Layers panel.

2. This opens the Layer Style dialog box and activates the Drop Shadow settings. The effect will be previewed on the document.

3. Apply the Structure and Quality settings as needed. Many times, all that is needed are minor tweaks to the Opacity, Angle, and Distance. Click OK when finished (**Figure 97b**).

(continued on next page)

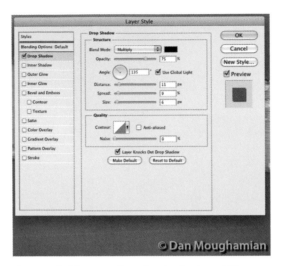

Figure 97b Minor tweaks to Opacity, Angle, and Distance will often provide a good result for a text-based drop shadow.

Blend Mode—This setting determines how the shadow will be blended with the background pixels. Because shadows are by definition dark, leaving this set to Multiple is usually a good idea.

Opacity—This setting determines the opacity or strength of the shadow.

Angle—This setting refers to the angle of the simulated light that is falling across the letters in your text and thus casting a shadow. Typically, values between 135 degrees and 45 degrees work best, in terms of maintaining readability and creating a pleasing look.

Distance—This setting defines the distance in pixels between the center point of the shadow text and the text layer itself. Usually, values between 4 and 10 pixels suffice for most photographic uses.

Spread—This setting is analogous to feathering a selection or mask; it tends to increase the width of the shadow's lettering or shape.

Size—This setting defines how large the shadow is. The larger you make it, the softer it becomes, and the less defined it becomes.

Quality—For text shadows, leave these settings to their default.

Layer Effects are like adjustment layers or Smart Filters in the sense that they are applied nondestructively.

#98 Printing Tips

There are a few settings in the Photoshop CS5 Print dialog box that you will want to be aware of when printing to photo inkjets. To open the Print dialog box (**Figure 98**), press Command-P (Mac OS) or Control-P (Windows).

Send 16-Bit Data   Color Settings

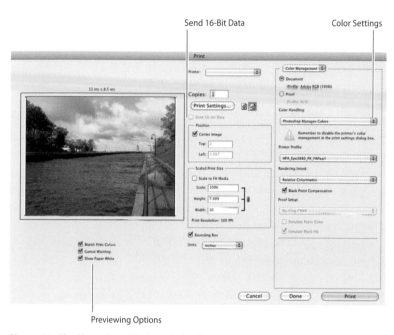

Previewing Options

Figure 98 The Photoshop CS5 Print dialog box.

Previewing

These settings help catch problems before you print, reducing the number of times you need to reprint after making adjustments.

Match Print Colors—Photoshop will attempt to match how it thinks the printed output will look, based on the settings you have chosen.

Gamut Warning—Photoshop will display as a solid color any regions in your image that it believes will not be faithfully reproduced by the printer and paper being used.

Show Paper White—This setting adjusts the preview to compensate for the difference between a monitor's white point and the white point of your target paper.

Color Settings

The settings that follow will go a long way toward determining how accurate the colors in your print turn out.

Send 16-bit Data—This setting is only available for the Mac OS. When selected, Photoshop will send 16-bit file data to the printer to aid in accurately reproducing areas with subtle gradation of tones (like blue skies). However, in practice, there is not always a noticeable difference between leaving this setting on or off; much depends on the image being printed, the paper, and especially the printer and its set of inks.

Color Handling—Choose Photoshop Manages Colors from this pop-up menu to ensure that Photoshop and not your printer's driver controls how colors are interpreted as part of the print process.

Printer Profile—Be sure to install and select a color profile that is specific to both your printer and the paper you are using. Here, I have a profile for Hahnemühle Fine Art Pearl Paper, specifically profiled for the Epson Stylus Pro 3880. If you use a profile other than one designed for both printer and paper type, you will likely get suboptimal results in many cases.

Rendering Intent—For most situations, if you have a professional ink-jet printer, you can leave the default settings (Relative Colorimetric and Black Point Compensation) active. If you have a less expensive printer, or are using less expensive paper, you may want to try Perceptual.

Print Settings

Every driver provides a slightly different layout and set of controls, depending on your OS and whether you have installed a driver from Apple, Microsoft, or the printer manufacturer. For this reason, it's difficult to speak generally about the settings to use, but there is one that universally should be turned off—your print driver's color management setting. As noted earlier, it's best to let Photoshop manage the color process, so any setting that indicates your printer is using color management by default should be turned off. On the Mac OS, this part of the driver is sometimes called ColorSync.

#99 Saving for the Web

Creating web-friendly versions of photographs is often an important task. To open the Save for Web & Devices window, choose File > Save for Web & Devices (**Figure 99**).

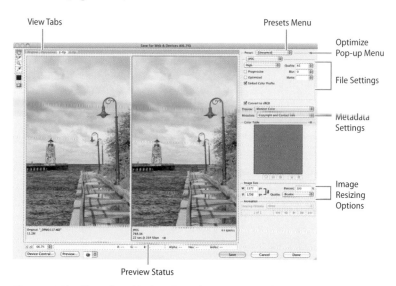

View Tabs

Presets Menu

Optimize Pop-up Menu

File Settings

Metadata Settings

Image Resizing Options

Preview Status

Figure 99 The Photoshop CS5 Save for Web & Devices window.

View Tabs

Near the top-left portion of the window there are four tabs. Each sets up the window for a different type of previewing. Original shows only the original file preview; Optimized shows only the preview with Save for Web & Devices settings applied; 2-Up will split the preview area in two views (as seen in Figure 99) and applies the Original preview to one pane and the Optimized preview to the second pane. There is also a 4-Up view that allows you to see three variations of the Optimized preview, each based on slightly different settings.

Image Sizing

In some cases for very high-resolution files, Save for Web & Devices may not be able to handle file-resizing tasks. For these cases, I typically default to using the Image > Image Size command.

Preview Stats

In 2-Up view, if you look below the bottom of the image preview, you will see the following information: Web File Format, File Size, and Time to View at a given download speed. On the right, you will see the Quality settings relative to the Web File Format being used (JPEG in Figure 99). If you click the pop-up menu to the right of the speed listing ("5 sec @ 384Kbps" in Figure 99), you will get a choice of speeds. The idea is that you can set that speed to see how quickly a viewer can download your file in a browser window.

File Settings

JPEG has been the almost universally adopted format by digital photographers who want to show still images online. The two most important settings are the Quality slider and the Convert to sRGB option. To avoid artifacts or color bands, a quality setting between 60 and 80 can be used to maintain a good balance between quality and file size.

Metadata Options

Under the Convert to sRGB option, there is a pop-up menu that contains different options for embedding and saving metadata with your web files. Typically, it's a good idea, assuming you've added the information using the steps discussed in Tip #60, to use either the Copyright or Copyright and Contact Information settings.

Image-Resizing Options

Here, you can choose the final web-output size for your files as an alternative to using the Image > Image Size command. Presuming your original file is much larger than that width, you can set the resizing Quality to Bicubic Sharper. When you click Save and give your new file a name, Photoshop will then automatically apply the quality settings, color space options, and metadata options and then resize the file before saving it.

Web Presets

Although I don't typically use the web presets that ship with Photoshop, I do find it useful to save my own presets. To save your JPEG settings (or other settings) as a web preset, click the Optimize pop-up menu (top-right corner) and choose Save Settings, then give them a name. Afterward your preset name will show up in the Preset pop-up menu.

#**100** Image Processor

At different times, you may be faced with the task of quickly processing and saving large numbers of raw files using the same setup. Handling each file manually would take far too much time, so Photoshop, Lightroom, and ACR all have their own versions of batch processing to speed these workflows. One of my favorites is the Image Processor in Photoshop because of its simplicity. To open the Image Processor choose File > Scripts > Image Processor and a straightforward dialog box will open (**Figure 100**). The Image Processor uses a labeled, 4-step process to help you get work done as efficiently as possible.

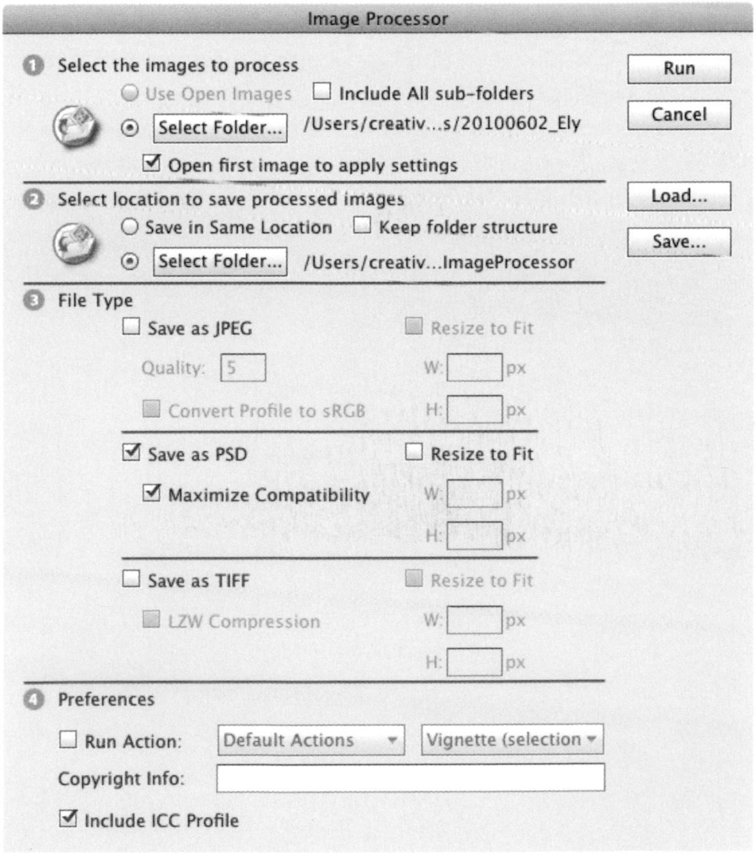

Figure 100 The Photoshop CS5 Image Processor allows you to define a target folder, create basic output settings, and quickly create a new set of images without having to create them manually.

Step 1 provides options for selecting the folder where your unprocessed images are stored and whether to process images that are found in subfolders. You also have the option to open the first image in ACR, ☑ Open first image to apply settings , so Photoshop can use that as a basis for settings to apply to the remaining photos.

Step 2 provides options for saving the processed files into the same source folder or a new folder that you define using standard file dialog boxes.

Step 3 defines which format your files will be saved to and whether to resize them as part of that process.

Step 4 allows you to run any custom actions you may have recorded, to add copyright information, and include an ICC color profile for color management.

When you're ready to run the processor, click the Run button. If you'd like to save your settings for use again later, click Save, and the Image Processor will create an XML file. Later, you can use the Load button to access the XML file and repopulate the settings.

Closing

There are of course many more capabilities and tips to be discovered when using Lightroom 3, Photoshop CS5, and ACR 6, but in any written work, the author must remain true to the scope and concept. I hope that you have found the scope of this book and the tips that I've chosen to be helpful, and that many of them will become an integral part of your digital photography process. It has been a pleasure (and an honor) to share these tips with you. Thank you for purchasing this book (I know you have many to choose from as there are many talented authors out there). I look forward to hearing from you. You can follow me (if you're into crazy mediums like Twitter) @Colortrails.

-Dan Moughamian
July 2010

Index